# THE
# RIGHT INSTRUMENT
# FOR YOUR CHILD

# THE
# RIGHT INSTRUMENT
# FOR YOUR CHILD

A practical Guide for
Parents and Teachers

## ATARAH BEN-TOVIM
### &
## DOUGLAS BOYD

LONDON
VICTOR GOLLANCZ LTD
1985

First published in Great Britain 1985
by Victor Gollancz Ltd,
14 Henrietta Street, London WC2E 8QJ

British Library Cataloguing in Publication Data
Ben-Tovim, Atarah
    The right instrument for your child.
    1. Instrumental music – Instruction and study
    I. Title    II. Boyd, Douglas
    780′.7′1        MT170

    ISBN 0 575 03489 0
    ISBN 0 575 03547 1 pbk

Designed by Leslie and Lorraine Gerry
Printed and bound in Great Britain
by Hazell  Watson & Viney Ltd, Aylesbury

# CONTENTS

# PART 1: YOUR CHILD

## How musical is your child?

Some parents take it for granted that their children are musical, while others believe that making music is an élite activity, restricted to talented or gifted children.

Most parents' view lies somewhere between the two extremes. They would like to inform themselves better. They would like to find someone whose business it is to answer questions such as:

"Are some children more musical than others?"

"Are some otherwise normal children so unmusical that they cannot learn to play an instrument?"

"What is the difference between the children who succeed in learning an instrument, and those who give up—the 'failures'?"

Although you can get advice from many sources—from school, from private music teachers, from other parents—the answers are often more confusing than the questions. It seems that the world is divided into those who can do it and those who can't, with no common language between them.

Many parents have themselves, as children, figured in the statistics of musical failure. Millions had piano lessons for months or even years, yet are now unable to read a note of music. Understandably, but wrongly, those people have come to believe that their failure to learn was due to some lack of musicality on their part.

Whichever kind of parent you are, you will find a wealth of help and advice in this book. It is written for parents by an ex-prodigy and an ex-failure! We stand on both sides of the musical divide. The prodigy was already playing concertos with professional symphony orchestras in her early teens; the drop-out gave up the piano after three years of agony,

and yet went on to spend twenty happy years in the music
business.

Because our own childhood experiences of music spanned
the gamut of publicly acclaimed success and privately demoralizing failure, we were interested both professionally
and personally to know whether children could be divided
into two convenient categories—"musical" and "unmusical"—as many teachers try to make us believe when they
attribute their terrible failure rate to such false reasons as
"the inevitable dropping-out of those not musical enough to
carry on". Also, we wanted to find out whether most
children who give up learning instruments do lack something
called "musicality". If they do, what exactly is it? If not,
what are the real reasons why they give up?

To avoid being influenced or biased by anyone or any
organization, we set up an independent Music Research
Centre in the North of England. There, and on our travels
throughout Britain and overseas, we interviewed several
thousand children who had given up learning instruments—
together with a control group who were continuing their
musical studies. Both groups were drawn from a wide range

of educational and social backgrounds. Some had learned in the traditional way, in private lessons, and some through the school system.

We found no evidence that the children who had given up learning were any less musical than their co-evals who were playing in school bands, County Youth Orchestras and so on. Perhaps even more surprisingly, other independent surveys have found that advanced music students in Music College and University are no more "musical" than their fellow-students reading Geography or Social Sciences. Why, then, do some drop out and some go on to succeed?

We found overwhelming evidence that the drop-outs had been wrongly advised, or encouraged, by adults to begin learning instruments on which they were individually bound for failure from the start. *Choosing the wrong instrument was the most common factor in musical failure—not lack of musicality, or musical potential.*

Who knows? If Yehudi Menuhin or John Williams had been made to learn the trumpet or drumkit originally, they too *might* have spent their adult lives listening to records and feeling unhappily that they had been cheated out of their musical birthright, "unable to play or read a note of music".

In our survey, we found that most physically and mentally normal children have musical potential far beyond what is necessary to learn to play the right instrument. However, a child set to learn a wrong instrument has to overcome a whole complex of unnecessary physical, mental and emotional handicaps. Taken together, these obstacles can more or less guarantee eventual failure on the instrument. Because it is so difficult for parent or child to unravel what went wrong, there is a tendency to settle for the simple—but damaging—explanation that the child was "just not musical enough" to learn.

We repeat that there are very few physically and mentally normal children who are not musical enough to learn the right instrument. Indeed, many handicapped children can make amazing progress on a properly selected instrument.

If you are a parent, it is one thing to read about children in general. We hope it is reassuring to you, to read about the thousands who took part in our ten-year research programme. However, your main interest is in *your* child. You want to be sure that he or she is musical enough to learn to play an instrument. Use the simple Musicality Test opposite. Don't be put off by its simplicity. It works.

*Circle round the appropriate answer.*

## Part A – Abilities

Can the child:

- recognize the theme music of favourite TV shows?    yes   no

- join in with "pop" at the right time when you sing Pop Goes The Weasel?    yes   no

- tell which is the high note when you sing HEE-HAW with HEE high and HAW low?    yes   no

- clap back to you a simple rhythm you tap out on the table? (Use the first two lines of Baa Baa Black Sheep)    yes   no

- identify correctly, with eyes closed, the sounds of you tapping (a) a glass and (b) a small saucepan? (Rehearse this with eyes open first.)    yes   no

- sing or whistle accurately a familiar TV theme, or song, when asked to do so?    yes   no

- complete the melody if you sing the first half of a known tune? (E.g. Parent: Baa baa black sheep, have you any wool?      Child: Yes sir, yes sir, three bags full.)    yes   no

- name three or more musical instruments?    yes   no

- name one, or more than one, instrumental musician?    yes   no

## Part B – Activities

Does the child:

- enjoy listening to music?    yes   no

- respond physically to music?    yes   no

- have some favourite music on record or cassette which he/she plays frequently?    yes   no

- repeatedly express a desire to play a certain instrument? (This will not necessarily be the right one.)    yes   no

If you have circled YES fewer than eight times, this does not necessarily mean that your child is unmusical. Most likely, he or she is too young—or too much occupied with school or other pressures—to begin developing musically.

In that case, do the Test again in about six months. Meanwhile, try to make a richer musical environment for the child. Invest in some favourite music on cassette. Watch musical programmes of all kinds on television, together with the child. Talk about what he or she likes and dislikes. If possible, take the child to some live events where musicians can be seen and heard—from circuses to brass bands to school concerts.

If you have circled YES eight or more times, your child is musical enough to learn to play an instrument.

Whether or not this musical potential is realized, depends on two things, both of them in your control:

  • choosing the right instrument, i.e. the one with no physical, mental or emotional problems for your child, and the maximum of physical, mental and emotional advantages;

  • starting to learn at the right time.

# Is your child ready to start learning an instrument?

Once you have established that your child is musical enough to learn to play an instrument, the next question to which you want an answer is: "When should he or she begin?" This is one of the questions most frequently asked by parents.

As a parent, you have watched your child develop physically, mentally and emotionally since birth. You have observed that every major achievement in your child's progress is made in its own good time. One child may walk before another, or talk before another. Yet, in each case, there are certain preparatory stages which have to be accomplished before the breakthrough to walking, talking, or whatever. To take one example, no child can walk upright before it has control of the right muscles and nerves. But it must also have a developed sense of balance. Otherwise, however strong the leg muscles, the child will fall.

Although you might find it difficult to put into words, you feel instinctively that a process as long and complicated as learning to make music on an instrument must also have a right time to begin. Because children do not all develop at the same speed, you accept that the right time for one may be wrong for another. Unfortunately, when parents put this question to teachers, they usually get unhelpful answers, which may leave the parent more confused than before. Some teachers will start children at any age. "The younger, the better!" they gaily cry. Some even insist that children must start to learn certain instruments, like the violin, at three or four—"before the bones have set". Yet, some school authorities recommend starting as late as thirteen or fourteen.

The parent comes to wonder whether to ignore the instinctive feeling that there must be some right time. It is tempting just to let the child begin when circumstances dictate. This is a great pity, because the parent was right.

*In all our thousands of interviews, the second most common factor in children's musical failure was starting at the wrong time—too early.*

Judging the right moment to begin is not simply a question of age. For one child it can be much earlier, or later, than for another. The right moment is a particular stage in your own child's physical, mental and emotional development. It is often later than you may have thought: for 95 per cent of children, the best time to start learning their first instrument is some time between the ages of eight and eleven.

Many parents throw up their hands in horror when they discover this. "Can't wait that long," they say. "Our six-year-old says every day: 'Mummy, I want to play the organ/flute/violin/guitar.' So, we're going to buy an instrument and start lessons—even if he is a bit young."

It is true that the six-year-old who goes on and on about wanting to play an instrument is experiencing the promptings of his developing instinct to make music. But he is not yet ready to do much about it. The instinct will naturally ebb and come back more strongly in a couple of years. What he actually feels is much too diffuse for any six-year-old to put into words, so he invents a specific achievement fantasy, and tells his parents: "I want to play the . . ."

Although it may sound to an adult ear like a mature decision to start all the hard work of learning an instrument, it should be treated more on the lines of: "I want to be a

racing driver/nurse/astronaut.''

"But, what about the five- and six-year-olds who do start learning and seem to make progress?" parents ask. In almost every case, these children are being "pushed" by a musically educated or musically frustrated parent, who attends lessons with the child and supervises daily practice in detail. The parent provides the motivation to begin and to continue, and tells the child what to do. Suzuki classes are an example. Unless you are that kind of parent, and intend to commit a regular part of every day to this shared musical education, day after day without respite for several years, it is not worth the extra risks of starting early.

Some parents wonder whether the child who starts proper instrumental lessons early will have some advantage, over those who begin later. The answer is: very little, if any. Remember that what takes a five-year-old three years to master can also be accomplished by an eight-year-old in a few months! So, use the Readiness Test. Like the Musicality Test, it looks simple, but it works.

It is not important how many YES's your child gets, but a single NO probably means that your child is not ready yet. If in any doubt, wait. Do not be tempted to cheat because your child has above-average school performance. The right moment is not just a question of intelligence; it is a coincidence of mental, physical and emotional development.

Can the child:

- already read and write fluently and with pleasure?   yes   no

- write correctly and without problems?   yes   no

- do simple addition, multiplication, subtraction and division sums?   yes   no

- cope emotionally with the social pressures of school (other children, teachers)?   yes   no

Has the child:

- attended full-time school for at least two and a half years?   yes   no

- carried on for six months or more any making or collecting hobby *or* regularly attended any out-of-school group or society for six months or more?   yes   no

Does the child:

- know the difference between work and play?   yes   no

- have the spare mental energy (after schoolwork is done) to begin an entirely new kinds of activity?*   yes   no

*Not the case, for example, within a year of changing school or starting secondary school.*

If you feel, after the Readiness Test, that your child is not quite ready to start formal lessons, it is always better to wait. But this waiting period does not have to be an empty one, for there is a suitable interim activity between playing at music and starting to learn an instrument properly. You can teach your child *basic* recorder technique.

Before you say: "Who, me? But I can't . . .", the answer is that you can. If children of six or eight are capable of learning to play simple tunes on the recorder, it stands to reason that any adult can teach him- or herself, in order to teach the child.

All you need to do, is buy a couple of recorders and a tutor book. You teach yourself one lesson ahead of the child, and off you go. So long as you treat the whole thing as fun and exciting—for both of you—you can do nothing but good.

Keep it fun. It is not necessary to push on to the next lesson in a hurry. Some children enjoy for months playing the same tunes. "Go and Tell Aunt Nancy" played for the thousandth time may drive you mad, but if that is the natural level of your child's musical ambition at present, you're right not to push him or her.

If interest does wane, it is probably because the child has come into another period of stress at school. Wait until the child has some more energy to spare, before you start again. In the meantime, you may have forgotten some of what was learnt, but the child will not have done.

At this stage, so long as it's fun, it's good.

## The systematic approach to finding the right instrument for your child

Now, you have reassured yourself that your child is musical enough to learn to play an instrument and you have checked that he or she is ready to begin. Naturally, you want to get to grips with the instruments and start ticking them off—"yes" to this one and "no" to that one. And so on. But, there is no hurry. Getting the selection right is one of the most important decisions you will ever make for, and with, your child.

If it is right, your child will enjoy a life-long enrichment of his or her life—the ability to make music, alone or with others, and to comprehend music more deeply than a non-player ever can. If it is wrong, he or she may well spend thousands of fruitless leisure hours frustrated at being unable to express the musical potential that you now know is there, waiting to be released. When you think how important leisure interests will be for your child's generation—with shorter working hours, high risk of redundancy and unemployment, a longer life-span but far earlier retirement—then you know how important it is to get this major decision right.

At this point, there are two ways in which you could select the instrument.

*There is the lazy way: the traditional hit-or-miss approach.* It misses far more often than it hits. You could start piano lessons because there is a teacher just round the corner. You could put the child's name down for free or subsidized lessons at school on whatever instrument happens to be available. The odds are about ten to one against your child succeeding.

What usually happens is that the child begins to learn with high hopes and true ambition. After a few months, the combined handicaps of the wrong instrument have so discouraged the child that he or she stops trying. Lessons continue because of pressure from the adults involved. A battle of wills develops between the increasingly unhappy child and the parents/teacher who use bullying, bribery and cajolery to ensure minimal practising and attendance at weekly lessons. No sane adult would try to make all children behave the same or decree that they should all wear the same size clothes, or all take up football, or all do knitting. Yet, when it comes to music it has so often been assumed that all children have the same aptitudes and needs, with millions of children set to learn piano or violin or other random instruments.

Because playing an instrument is a deeply personal activity, this random imposition of instruments leaves the child with only one way of demonstrating his or her individuality: negatively. The child becomes "difficult", refuses to practise, skips lessons and eventually gives up.

Anyone can see that this is a waste of the child's time— and probably the parent's money as well. What is not so obvious is that the child feels a deep sense of failure which lingers for many years, has learnt that he or she is "no good at music", and feels cheated. Learning blocks develop, which can affect schoolwork adversely. When you add all this up, it is a heavy price to pay for being in a hurry and not spending enough time  choosing the instrument methodically in the first place.

*The other way of choosing the instrument is the systematic one: dealing with each aspect of the choice, separately and logically.*

To do this, you need a system which unravels all the problems, puts them in the right order and gives you the information which you need to come to the right decision. That is what this book is. There are very few DO's and DON'T's, because you, the parent, are in charge. All we do is to set out the problems for you, indicate the order in which they should be tackled—and give you all the information you need.

# Ben-Tovim/Boyd system

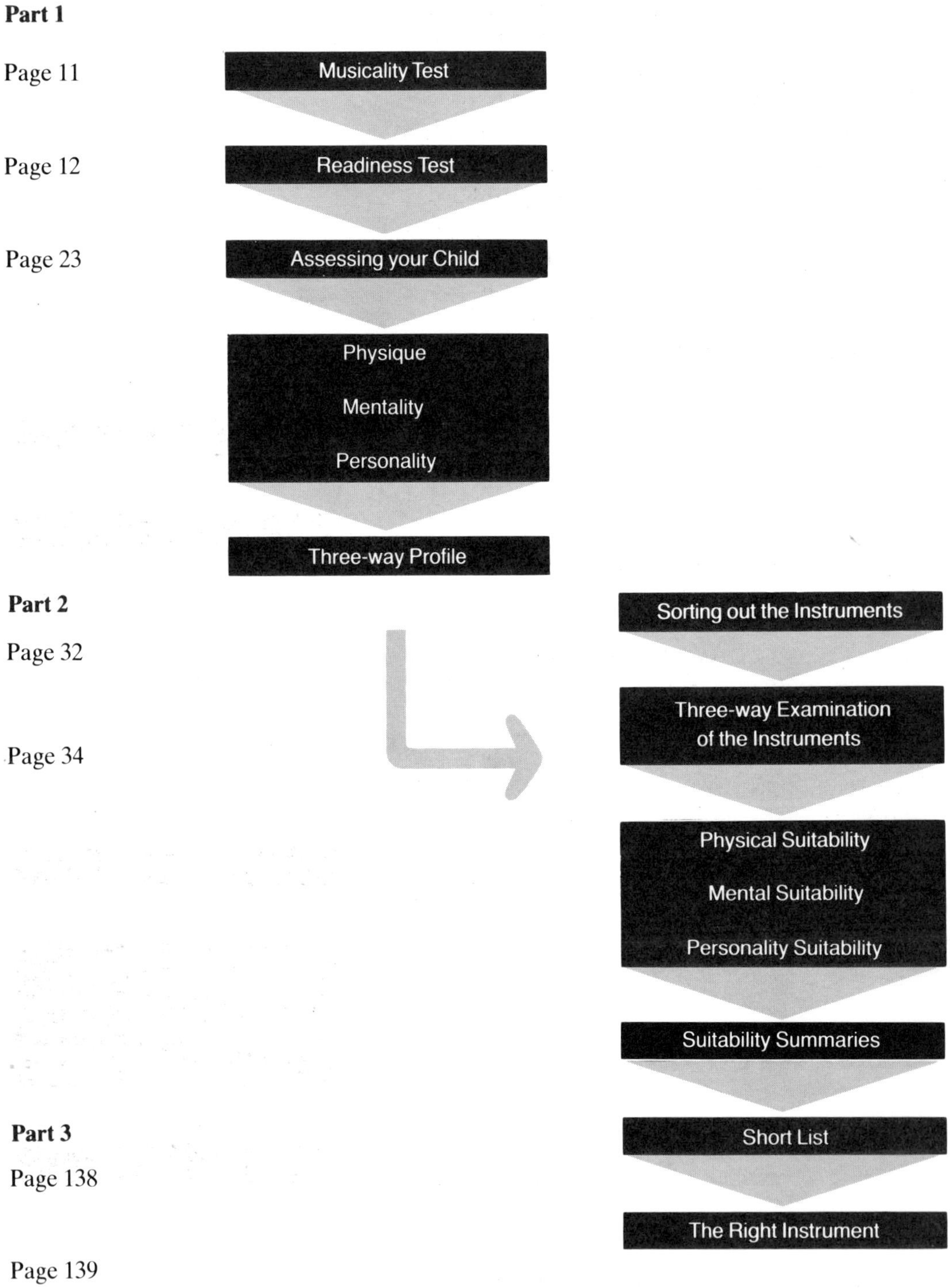

**Part 1**

Page 11

| Musicality Test |

Page 12

| Readiness Test |

Page 23

| Assessing your Child |

| Physique |
| Mentality |
| Personality |

| Three-way Profile |

**Part 2**

Page 32

| Sorting out the Instruments |

Page 34

| Three-way Examination of the Instruments |

| Physical Suitability |
| Mental Suitability |
| Personality Suitability |

| Suitability Summaries |

**Part 3**

Page 138

| Short List |

Page 139

| The Right Instrument |

It does not matter how much or how little you know about music. This book is the result of a unique programme of research during which the writers personally counselled several thousand parents and children who came from many countries for help in finding the right instrument. Every piece of advice in the book has been tried and tested many times in consultation with teachers, psychologists, musicians, doctors, dentists, youth workers and other specialists.

Our system has nothing to do with producing prodigies or turning out professional musicians. So, you can forget anything you may vaguely remember about prodigies and professionals. Also, take no notice of friends, relatives or teachers who try to persuade you that what was right for another child must somehow be right also for your child.

Prodigies and professionals are not important, or relevant. Not even the instruments are important. Your child is important. So, our system is child-centred.

This is how it works:

The first stage is to make sure that the child is musical enough to learn an instrument.

Since most children who fail began at the wrong time, you need to check that your child is ready to begin learning.

| Musicality Test |
| Readiness Test |

Playing an instrument is a physical activity, but it also involves the player's intelligence and uses his or her feelings, or emotions.

Your child is not a carbon copy of any other child. He or she is a unique combination of physical, mental and emotional characteristics.

To find the instrument which requires the aptitudes your child has, and fulfils his or her needs, it is necessary to be very objective and clear in assessing his or her ● ● ● ●

| Assessing your Child |
| Physique |
| Mentality |
| Personality |
| Three-way Profile |

This gives you a Three-Way Profile of your child: a

description which covers all those characteristics that govern the choice of instrument.

Only after assessing your child in these three ways, is it time to begin thinking about the instruments.

First, they are sorted into the recognized groups, or families, of allied instruments. All the instruments in a group share certain important characteristics.

In Part 2 of this book, you will find comprehensive information about all the instruments—including some you might not otherwise have thought about.

The information is set out clearly and objectively, taking into account the physical, mental and emotional requirements, and rewards, of each instrument.

You examine each one for suitability for your child, using the Three-Way Profile of your child ● ● ● ● ● ●

At the end of the information about each instrument, there is a Suitability Summary, which you complete by putting a tick or a cross against each of the three headings: Physical, Mental and Personality.

Some instruments resolve themselves easily; others take a little time. But *the system works for you*, so that eventually you have only a few Suitability Summaries which have no cross on them.

These instruments are the "possibles" for your child. They make up his or her ● ● ● ● ● ● ● ● ●

Checking through the instruments on the Short List is done mainly with the child. Because of the systematic way in which you have arrived at the Short List, you will feel secure and unhurried, when it comes to making the final selection. All the information you need is in Part 3.

Sorting out the Instruments

Three-way Examination
of the Instruments

Physical Suitability

Mental Suitability

Personality Suitability

Suitability Summaries

Short List

The Right Instrument

## Assessing your child

There are two kinds of knowledge you need, in order to make the right choice of instrument for your child. Certainly, you need to know about *all* the instruments—in terms of the physical, mental and emotional requirements they make on the player and the physical, mental and emotional rewards they offer in return.

However, the more important body of knowledge is about your child. You, the parent, are the expert in this. You know more about your child than anyone else. You can assess your child better than any musician or teacher could hope to do.

So, why do you need help from us? And why should you have to draw up something which sounds as complicated as a Three-Way Profile of your child's physical, mental and emotional (or personality) characteristics?

Because playing an instrument is not quite like any other activity your child has undertaken.

The classroom should develop the brain, but does nothing for the emotions. Sports concentrate on physical development. Other activities may stimulate emotions, but do not seem to develop mentality or physique. Only music activates and develops your child's body, brain and emotional personality in a balanced and synchronized way. Whether you would choose to put it in those words or not, that is the real reason why you want your child to learn to play an instrument.

The right instrument has to match your child's body, brain and emotions. It is no use finding an instrument that suits the body if the child is sociable and the instrument is a solitary, or self-contained one—like guitar or piano. It is no use finding an instrument whose music suits the mentality, if the child has not the body to enjoy playing it. The right instrument must match the child in all three ways: physique, mentality and personality.

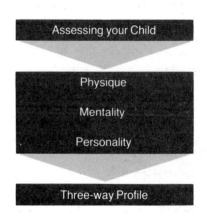

But, which are the parts of the body, and what are the aspects of mentality and personality, which govern the choice of instrument?

Instead of giving you an academic answer, which would sound very clever, but actually be rather confusing, we include on the following pages three polarization charts. These were drawn up by the team of specialist advisers we work with. By using them, you ensure that your child's Three-Way Profile embraces all those characteristics which are important.

The first chart covers the physical characteristics which are involved in playing instruments. It is perhaps the easiest chart to use, for every parent knows whether the child is over-weight or has long arms, lacks some second teeth, etc.

The second and third charts, which deal with mentality and personality (the kind of child), will take more time. It can be useful to look at school reports, but you should take into account equally the child's attitudes and behaviour in the home, in hobbies, in leisure activities.

A child does *not* have to be good at school, in order to succeed on the right instrument. Most schools and teachers denigrate those characteristics which make life in the class-room more difficult—so that IMPATIENT, SLOW-LEARNING, CAN'T CONCENTRATE are criticized as defects—when they are really no more than indicators of how the child reacts to the classroom. In some cases, the very characteristics which school-teachers most dislike can lead to success in learning the right instrument.

Often, too, the children most under-valued at school make excellent progress on an instrument—partly because they have been denied achievement in the classroom. Happily this, in its turn, helps them to cope with the problems they formerly had at school.

All you have to do, to make up your child's profile, is to circle round the words on the charts which apply to your child. There are no "right" or "wrong" answers. There are no points to score. But, you must be objective. Gentle cheating—to make a nicer or more favourable picture of the child—is a natural temptation for a parent. Resist it!

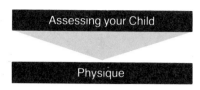

*Circle round the words that apply to your child*

| | | | |
|---|---|---|---|
| Eyesight | excellent | normal | astigmatic / wears spectacles |
| Hearing | acute | normal | below normal |
| Lips | thin | average | thick |
| Mouth control | can whistle | | can't whistle |
| Front teeth | protruding | normal | receding |
| Front teeth | large | average | small |
| Front teeth | even and regular | | irregular |
| Dental development | first teeth | second teeth coming through | second teeth firm in gums |
| Lungs/breathing | asthmatic/bronchitic | average | strong |
| Reach of arms | short | average for height | long |
| Hand-span | Can span an octave on piano | | can't span an octave* |
| Fingers | short | average | long |
| Little finger | short | average | long |
| Breadth of finger pads | narrow | average | broad |
| Dexterity | left-handed | | right-handed |
| Physical co-ordination | clumsy | normal | well co-ordinated |
| Physical energy | energetic | average | sedentary |
| Physical energy | enjoys sports | not sporting | lacks energy |
| General health | delicate | normal | robust |
| General physique | tall | average for age | short |
| General physique | over-weight | average | thin |
| Physical feeling | likes putting things in mouth | | does not like it |
| Physical feeling | likes vibration against lips† | | does not like it |

*7½ inches or 19 centimetres
†such as a kazoo, or comb and tissue paper

26

Assessing your Child

Mentality

*Circle round the words that apply to your child*

| Mental type | logical/mathematical | | intuitive/artistic | |
|---|---|---|---|---|
| Speed of learning | quick | average | slow | |
| Memory | good | average | finds memorising difficult | |
| Reading | reads habitually, for pleasure | can read fluently | not fluent | |
| Writing | fluent | | not fluent | |
| Mathematics | likes the subject | can do it | has problems | |
| Mental arithmetic | finds it easy | average | finds it hard | |
| Concentration | daydreams often | average | concentrates well | |
| Persistence | needs quick results | | prepared to "plod along" | |
| Attitude to schoolwork | has problems | | no problems at school | |
| School achievement | near top of class | average | below average | |
| Application | lazy | works if pushed | conscientious | |
| Spare mental energy after school | plenty | some | none | |

**Personality**

*Which of these alternatives describes your child? Circle them*

| | | |
|---|---|---|
| generous | or | acquisitive |
| a few special friends | or | many friends |
| calm | or | lively |
| bright, quick-witted | or | dreamy, forgetful |
| quiet | or | boisterous |
| some hobbies | or | no leisure interests |
| solitary | or | sociable, gregarious |
| prefers physical activity | or | prefers mental activities |
| outgoing | or | shy |
| enjoys relating to adults | or | doesn't enjoy relating to adults |
| likes parents to be involved | or | likes to be independent of family |
| easy-going | or | ambitious |
| determined | or | gives up easily |
| self-centred | or | sensitive to others |
| academic | or | creative |
| patient | or | impatient |
| attention-seeking | or | prefers not to be noticed |
| dominant, bossy | or | responsive, likes others to lead |
| peaceable | or | aggressive |
| soft, gentle | or | hard, tough |
| moody | or | even-tempered |
| casual | or | intense |
| serious | or | fun-seeking |
| self-disciplined | or | fidgetty |
| responsible | or | doesn't like responsibility |
| good-natured | or | has fits of temper |
| "difficult" | or | well-balanced |
| stubborn | or | easily led |
| good at modelling or needlework | or | "bad with hands" |

*Note:*
*This chart can be difficult to use because your child's personality interacts with your own in normal family life. Two adult brains may be better than one, to obtain objectivity.*

By indicating those words on the three charts which apply to your child, you have made a Three-Way Profile. It summarizes all the information about the child necessary before you begin to think about the instruments, and to cross-refer to, as you work through them, one by one.

In the second part of this book, you will discover thousands of facts about the various instruments. Most of these facts are unknown even to professional teachers and musicians—because music teachers and musicians are almost all specialists. Each knows a lot about one instrument and a certain amount about the rest of the group to which that instrument belongs. Musicians' training makes them very specialist and narrow. Rarely will a flute-player, for example, know anything useful about percussion—or a brass-player about the strings, or the guitar.

That is why parents who go to a teacher or a musician and ask for advice in finding an instrument get wrong answers. In ninety-nine cases out of a hundred, the musician or teacher will suggest either his own instrument or another which belongs to the same group. This does not mean that he has the remotest idea what is suitable; it means simply that his knowledge is limited.

The only person who has a reasonably comprehensive knowledge of many instruments is the orchestral conductor. He knows a lot about the instruments of the orchestra, but he does not necessarily know anything about non-orchestral instruments. Nor would he be able to advise about the instruments in terms of their usefulness to your child, because that is not his job.

By the time you have worked through to the end of this book, *you* will be the person best equipped to find the right instrument for your child. You are already the expert on your child. All the expertise you need about the instruments is in Part 2.

PART 2: THE INSTRUMENTS

Any reasonably large music shop offers you today a range of instruments at prices suitable for children to learn on—a range which is larger than ever before. This is because modern methods of instrument manufacture have actually reduced the real cost of most student instruments.

Of course, that is a good thing, but many parents find the sheer extent of the range of instruments disturbing. They are tempted to seek refuge in the much smaller range of instruments which are familiar: piano, violin, guitar and maybe, flute.

If you are one of these parents who would feel at a disadvantage on walking into a music shop and being confronted by shelves and showcases full of instruments, use our simple system to sort them all out.

The instruments are like a pack of cards. In the same way

that it can be difficult to distinguish one instrument from another when they are all jumbled together in a shop, so it is hard to check that all the cards are there—and none missing—if the pack has been scattered at random across the table.

What do you do? You separate the cards into their four suits, and then make sure you have all the cards in each suit. If there are some jokers or other odd cards, you deal with them last.

That system works just as well for sorting out the instruments. There are four suits, or main groups, of instruments:

- the Woodwind
- the Brass
- the Stringed Instruments
- the Percussion.

The "jokers" are:

- the Self-Contained Instruments
- the Self-Taught Instruments.

# How to examine the instruments

Three-way Examination
of the Instruments

Physical Suitability

Mental Suitability

Personality Suitability

Suitability Summaries

Three-way Examination
of the Instruments

Physical Suitability

All the instruments have one thing in common: they were designed, or evolved, as machines to be operated by the body of a fully-grown man. No instrument was designed to be operated by the body of a six-year-old, or even an eleven-year-old child.

Some instruments are highly-developed machines—such as the piano which does most of the physical work for the player. Only three instruments are made in small sizes: the violin, guitar and cello. (For technical reasons, other instruments would not function properly if their sizes were reduced.) Yet, size and physical ease of operation do not make any instrument automatically suitable for children. In fact, the piano, violin and guitar are among the most difficult instruments to learn—and have the highest failure rates.

It is a coincidence if your child's body happens to be able to play an instrument designed for Dad to play. Some instruments are too heavy, or too large, or require too much physical energy for your child to play them. True, some other children may play them, but your child would be uncomfortable, or even stressed, trying to play these instruments. Why should any child—or adult—go on doing something which is uncomfortable, or stressful? Physical discomfort is a great reason for giving up an instrument.

So, first and foremost, the right instrument is one which is physically comfortable for the child to hold and play—because he or she happens to have the developed physical characteristics which are important for playing that instrument.

This physical matching is not just a question of the child fulfilling the requirements of the instrument. In return, the child *must* get certain physical rewards.

Playing any instrument has a particular sensation, because of the way in which the player's body is used in the process of playing. We call this "physical feed-back". Some children like the feed-back, or sensation, of playing the violin; others are left cold by it. Some children like the feeling of an oboe or clarinet reed vibrating in the mouth; others hate it.

*Physical Suitability* is a compound: the child fulfils the requirements of the instrument without stress or discomfort; in return, the child gets the reward of a physical feed-back which he or she finds pleasurable. Physical pleasure from playing the instrument is the most powerful reason of all why a child should carry on learning.

### The right instrument gives the child physical pleasure, without stress or discomfort

You can see at a glance that the physical requirements of playing, say, the flute and the double bass are very different. Whilst you cannot see the difference in mental requirements of the various instruments, they are equally important.

Playing a single-note instrument, such as cornet or flute, requires far less mental energy than a chordal instrument such as guitar or piano. Yet, a mechanically simple old instrument such as the violin demands vastly more mental energy than the recently invented saxophone.

Some children have a brain which does one thing at a time. They may be very fast movers, but they actually deal with one thing at a time. Other children, who may be good at mental arithmetic or chess, find pleasure in complexity— dealing with several things apparently at the same moment. One-thing-at-a-timers find their pleasure on single-note instruments, while those who are top of the class at mental arithmetic find the complexity of the chordal instruments a satisfying, but never demoralizing, challenge.

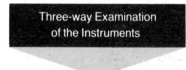

Three-way Examination
of the Instruments

Mental Suitability

**The right instrument gives the child no mental stress, but the continuing stimulation of doing something which his or her brain finds natural**

The third way in which an instrument must suit the child involves the emotions, or personality, of the player. This may sound a little diffuse, but the information about each instrument is set out so that this aspect is no more difficult to deal with than the other two.

Certain instruments suit certain kinds of children. Hyperactive children are a nightmare for a violin teacher, but a dream for percussionists. The very sound made by an instrument appeals more to certain children than to others. A gentle, wistful child drawn to the sound of the viola would be unhappy on the oboe and probably could not play the trumpet without pain.

Some instruments are solitary. A sociable, outgoing child who is learning classical guitar or piano, is bound to be frustrated and unhappy because he will have no chance of playing with others for many years to come. Conversely, a truly solitary child will be miserable on a brass instrument, which is used for making music only in bands or orchestras.

**Three-way Examination of the Instruments**

**Personality Suitability**

**The right instrument satisfies and develops the emotional side of the child's nature and does not frustrate it**

The Three-Way Profile of your child makes it easy and uncomplicated to examine the physical, mental and personality requirements and rewards of the instruments, one by one.

At the end of the information about each instrument, there is a  •  •  •  •  •  •  •  •  •  •  •  •  •  •

**Suitability Summary**

It is worth filling in all the Suitability Summaries, even if you have already decided in your own mind that the instruments in a particular group are inappropriate.

Do put a cross against any aspect of an instrument which does not suit your child.

DON'T be tempted to put a tick, if you are less than certain it is right.

DON'T WORRY if you feel that you ought to leave some squares blank. For, example, it may be difficult to decide on physical feed-back until the child has had the opportunity of holding the instrument and going through the motions of playing. These DON'T KNOWS resolve themselves automatically later on.

# Thinking about the Woodwind

The woodwind instruments are all pipes which you blow to play tunes. Flute, oboe and clarinet are high or treble instruments; the bassoon is a low, bass instrument. The saxophones and recorders range from high to low.

Parents know that most modern children want quick results. In musical terms, today's children want to make a nice sound and be able to play tunes in a few months.

The flute and clarinet figure on more shortlists than any other instruments because they (and, for older children, the saxophones, too) give this kind of rapid achievement. The oboe and bassoon do not.

The woodwind instruments play only one note at a time. So, the written music is neither difficult to read, nor is a good memory required. These instruments do so much of the work of making the sound that no especial musicality or even good sense of pitch is required. Many children who cannot sing a tune perfectly can learn to play a flute or clarinet quite well.

Little parental involvement is called for by children learning to play these instruments, apart from natural encouragement and support.

All this group of instruments were, as the name tells us, originally made of wood and powered by wind, i.e. the controlled breath of the player. Today, oboes, clarinets and bassoons are still made of wood or plastic, but most flutes are now made of metal. The saxophones are late-comers to the woodwind family and have always been made of brass. Piccolo, cor anglais, E Flat clarinet, bass clarinet and contra bassoon also belong to the woodwind but are not for beginners. Fifes and penny whistles, etc., also belong to this group.

Although these instruments are grouped together for convenience, the "feed-back" of playing them differs considerably. There is little similarity between the feeling of blowing *over* the open hole of a flute and forcing air *through* the narrow reed of the oboe; or between the way in which the lips are folded tightly over the teeth to grip the oboe reed and the manner in which the clarinet mouthpiece is thrust right into the mouth. Few children will be attracted equally to flute and clarinet; if they really like one, they won't like the other very much. Very few children will want to play the oboe or the bassoon.

Children who have enjoyed playing the recorder either in school or at home are naturally attracted, as they grow older and bigger, to the *apparently* similar instruments in the woodwind group. Parents should bear in mind that learning the recorder is an excellent training for *any* instrument. The fact that a child has enjoyed the recorder when young should not restrict the choice of the second instrument only to the woodwind family, even though the flute or the clarinet will almost certainly appear on that child's shortlist.

Children today spend a lot of time *sitting* in school, in vehicles, watching television and so on. Playing a woodwind or a brass instrument expresses some of the otherwise unused physical energy, whilst not demanding a great deal of sheer strength.

As to price, oboes and saxophones may seem expensive and bassoons *are* very expensive, but beginners' flutes and clarinets cost little more than a teenager's bicycle and have the advantage that, like all instruments, they hold their value well for possible re-sale or trade-in.

# FLUTE

Children like the sound of the flute, the notes first learned lying in the register of a ten-year-old's voice. It is an instrument designed to play tunes on. Playing tunes, or singing them, is the way in which a child naturally expresses his or her musical instincts. Hence, the appeal of the flute.

The flute appeals more strongly to girls than to boys.

Flutes of one kind or another have been used for playing tunes for many thousands of years, all over the world. The orchestral flute, as we know it, is a reedless instrument, held horizontal to the right side of the body. Sound is produced by pursing the lips and blowing a controlled stream of air across the open hole of the head-joint—rather like blowing over a pen-top or the head of a milk bottle. This sounds—and is—simple, but some children do not have the necessary lip-control to do it. The flute is not for them.

The keywork on a modern flute may look complicated, but the golden rule with instruments is: *the more complicated they are as machines, the easier they are to play* (a very simple instrument like the violin leaves all the work to the player, while the mechanically more complicated flute or clarinet does much of the work for you, so progress in learning can be rapid).

Within weeks, a beginner can progress from playing notes, and the satisfaction of producing a nice and musical sound, to playing simple tunes from ear and written music.

The flute comes into three pieces and fits into a small carrying case. It is easily put together and can be played and practised anywhere, better standing than seated.

Fingering is similar to that for the recorder, which gets recorder-players off to a flying start!

## Physical Suitability

Many young children are attracted to the flute and want to begin learning it long before their bodies are ready. Unlike the violin or the guitar, which are available in small sizes for beginners, it is not possible to make a reduced-size wind instrument, for technical reasons. (The piccolo is not a small-size flute; it is a different instrument.) Therefore, the body of a child playing the flute has to do the same work as that of an adult flautist, for whose much larger body the instrument was designed.

A single look at most young children playing the flute demonstrates the problem: in order to reduce the distance which the left arm has to stretch, the flute is not held horizontal, as it should be. This in turn means that the neck has to be twisted and the head held crooked in order to keep the lips at right angles to the flute.

The "right age to begin playing the flute" is when the child can stand upright, with the neck straight, and hold the flute horizontal, with the left arm comfortably stretched across the chest. As long as a child has to twist the head and neck in order to reduce the left-arm stretch, he or she is too small to start playing the flute.

Because there is no reed on the flute to produce the basic sound, the shape of the lips is very important. Thick lips or

very thin lips are not advised. Large upper front teeth are a handicap.

There is little obvious feedback when trying out the flute in a music shop. The feedback from playing comes after a few minutes of blowing: the flute uses so much air that playing it is like continuously blowing up balloons—it can make you very dizzy and even nauseated. Frail children find this unpleasant. Robust children enjoy it.

Boys and girls who like the feeling of moving to music, in dance or ballet, feel good playing the flute in a standing position, which is how it should always be practised.

The flute is the only instrument held far out to the side of the body. It is so designed that it can only be held to the right. This makes it a difficult instrument for complete left-handers who have an insufficient awareness of what is going on on the right side of their bodies.

The player cannot see his or her fingers whilst playing; because there is no visual check on what the fingers are doing and because playing the flute uses all eight fingers and the left thumb, a child with any problem or difficulty in controlling and co-ordinating the fingers will not be happy on the flute.

## Mental Suitability

The flute suits a wide range of mental ability: comparatively slow learners happily spend months, even years, learning to play simple tunes beautifully; quick learners race ahead, extending technique, increasing speed and progressing to increasingly difficult studies and repertoire.

Flute music is easy to read, so flute-players do not need particularly good memories.

## Personality Suitability

Shy or lonely children (who enjoy their own privacy) adore playing tunes on their flutes day after day, week after week.

But quietly sociable children are equally happy to find that, after about a year of learning properly, they can make music together with their friends in self-organized groups *and* be welcome in almost every kind of supervised music-making-ensembles, orchestras and bands of all kinds.

Probably the only kind of child who can find no satisfaction on this instrument is the aggressive or dominant child who needs to expend more energy and produce more noise than the flute will allow.

| Suitability Summary | ✓ or ✗ |
| --- | --- |
| Physical | |
| Mental | |
| Personality | |

43

# CLARINET

At a casual glance, the clarinet may look similar to the recorder. In fact, it is very different in almost every respect.

To produce a sound on the recorder, you place the mouthpiece between your lips and simply blow into it. On the clarinet, the sound is produced by the player thrusting the mouthpiece inside the mouth and holding it with the front upper teeth while blowing to vibrate the wide reed which is clamped to the mouthpiece, a process similar to the way in which children make a squeaky noise by vibrating a blade of grass stretched between the thumbs.

Vibrating the clarinet reed can produce a surprising volume of sound for little effort. However, the vibration of the reed inside the mouth produces a very strong feedback of which the player cannot be unaware.

Many boys are drawn to the instrument because it can make such a "big sound" and also because the notes first learned correspond to the slightly lower register of a boy's voice.

Its design gives the clarinet a great range of notes, which enables it to play, and be a solo instrument in, many kinds of music.

Alone among the woodwind, the clarinet has its own system of fingering, but this is not a problem, except initially for children who have played the recorder previously. (All the other woodwind use a modified system of recorder fingering.)

Most children find it easy to produce a sound on the clarinet, find the fingering logical and are reassured by being able to see their hands whilst playing.

Parents are amazed how quickly their children can make progress on this instrument. Within a few weeks, they can play tunes. Within months, they are ready to join a school band or orchestra.

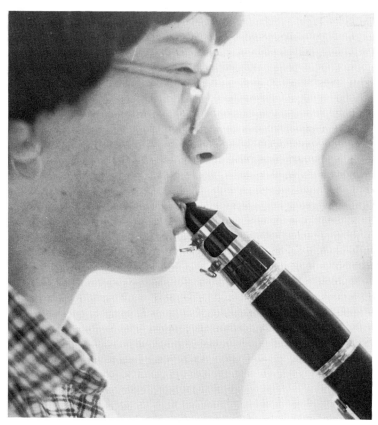

## Physical Suitability

To play the clarinet, the player inserts the mouthpiece, to which the reed is fastened, right into the mouth. Some children find the sensation of the reed vibrating inside the mouth very satisfying; for others, it is like trying to play a dentist's drill!

It is easier to make a sound on the clarinet than on the flute, for the reed does some of the work for you. Strong front teeth which would be a nuisance on the flute are a positive advantage on the clarinet. On the other hand a child who has had the adenoids removed would probably be unable to obtain sufficient breath-compression to play comfortably.

The playing position is comfortable for most nine- or ten-year-olds, with the hands clearly in view in front of the body.

Make sure that (a) fingers can span the distance between the keys, which is greater than on the flute, (b) pads of the finger-tips are broad enough to cover the open-hole keys.

## Mental Suitability

Quick learners and impatient children enjoy the rapidity of progress on the clarinet.

The music is not difficult to read but the great range of the instrument means that it is harder to read and play clarinet music than music for flute or oboe.

Also, because each note has its own fingering on the clarinet (for technical reasons), it demands a higher degree of finger co-ordination and control. Boys with a passion for model-making and taking things to pieces have developed this set of skills better than most girls.

Advanced clarinet playing can be stimulating for a mentally agile child as it involves the use of two instruments and sometimes transposition.

## Personality Suitability

Clarinet children tend to have several different hobbies or interests and flit from one to another. They are bright and alert, whereas a flute child may seem dreamy and forgetful.

The clarinet tends to suit sociable children rather than those who want to play on their own. After acquiring a basic competence on the instrument, most clarinettists become bored with their own company and look forward to the prospect of playing with others in orchestras, bands or clarinet choirs.

| Suitability Summary | ✓ or ✗ |
| --- | --- |
| Physical | |
| Mental | |
| Personality | |

# SAXOPHONE

These instruments are often overlooked by parents, yet for children who do not like classical music and do not want to play in formal orchestras or chamber groups they have a lot to offer.

There are four different saxophones: soprano, alto, tenor and baritone (rather like the four different recorders). Older children with a good sense of rhythm can get a lot of fun from the alto or tenor sax.

Of all instruments, the saxophones come closest to the sound of the human voice—not the high, piping voice of a little child, maybe, but certainly from early adolescence onwards. Boys as their voices break and girls who grow tall tend to find that they outgrow any natural desire to make the clean treble sound of recorder or flute but are attracted to the lower, throaty sound of the alto and tenor saxes. Conversely, few young children or small-bodied girls will naturally like the sound of these instruments.

The fingering is similar to that for recorder, flute and oboe. Thus, children who want to change from these other woodwind instruments, transfer happily and quickly to the sax, feeling that what they have previously learned has not been wasted. The freedom available to sax-players improvising in jazz and dance bands appeals to teenagers who want to express their personalities or be more "creative" than is possible playing written music in an orchestra.

Saxophones are expensive—around twice the cost of flute or clarinet.

## Physical Suitability

Few children start to play the saxes before the age of twelve or thirteen. The playing position is quite comfortable by this age, with the weight of the instrument (saxophones are heavy!) largely borne by the sling around the player's neck. Although much larger than flutes, oboes and clarinets, the saxophones, being of recent invention, are designed to be easier to operate. No great hand-stretches are involved, but, as hands are out of sight—except on the soprano sax which is small enough to be held in front of the body—reasonable finger co-ordination is called for.

The large mouth-piece inserted into the player's mouth produces a vibration feed-back similar to that of the clarinet and calls for strong or large teeth and generous lips.

## Mental Suitability

Quick results for all! Much easier to learn than flute or clarinet. The sax is easy to play and the music not difficult to read. Satisfying progress is made without much practising.

## Personality Suitability

These instruments suit children who may have been labelled "casual" or "fails to concentrate" but are by no means dull. Happy, well-balanced gregarious players, who do not want a close relationship with a teacher, find the saxes an ideal way of getting out into the world and making music with friends—and making friends with music.

Adolescents who already play one, or more, classical instruments (such as piano and violin) are often attracted to the sax because it promises such relief from the inhibitions of written music and formal style. For them, the sax is a fun instrument: easy to learn, loud—and designed for the delicious freedom of improvisation.

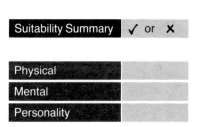

| Suitability Summary | ✓ or ✗ |
| --- | --- |
| Physical | |
| Mental | |
| Personality | |

In the hands of an outstanding professional musician playing chamber or orchestral music, the oboe can sound exquisite. Played by most children who are learning, the sound is unpleasing and rasping, which offers little encouragement to the player or to other members of the family within earshot. If your child is vaguely thinking about the oboe, or the school is trying to persuade her to take it up and play in the orchestra, there is only one word of advice: Don't!

The only children who can enjoy learning this instrument are those who, for a complex of reasons difficult for the outsider—even a parent—to unravel, simply know a hundred per cent that this is the instrument for them. It is self-selecting in every sense, usually by girls about twelve or thirteen who have learned to read music on a previous instrument and like the sound, or the idea, of playing in the woodwind section of an orchestra sufficiently to justify the long devotion and hard practice necessary to make any progress.

Fingering is similar to that of the recorder and flute, but the lip technique is extremely difficult to acquire.

## Physical Suitability

The most important physical requirement is the shape of the lips: they must be thin and tight, capable of being folded over the teeth to grip the narrow reed which is inserted into the mouth. The vibration of the reed within the mouth when playing is a feeling which some children like; others it makes squeamish.

The aperture between the two pieces of reed is so tight that the player has to *force* the breath through. Children may experience headaches from the back-pressure which this causes, even in a healthy teenager.

Not an instrument for frail children: the breath control is harder for the oboe than for any other wind instrument and so it must not be attempted unless the child is physically fit, even athletic—and the older the better. The oboe should never be played or even practised by any adolescent with a head-cold, respiratory or virus infection. The inter-cranial pressure can spread the infection into the eyes and the brain causing complications and even permanent disability.

## Mental Suitability

Impossible to generalize! There are no quick results but, any *determined* learner with the *sheer willpower* to succeed and the necessary motivation can make progress.

## Personality Suitability

The oboe is not for generous extroverts; determined, tight-lipped, stubborn children do best. A strong and close relationship with the teacher is called for in order to make progress. Insecure or intense adolescents often benefit by forming this kind of relationship with an adult outside the family.

Oboists tend not to mix well but to have one or two close friends. Even in an orchestral woodwind section, the oboe-players make a little clan and keep to themselves.

| Suitability Summary | ✓ or ✗ |
|---|---|
| Physical | |
| Mental | |
| Personality | |

53

## BASSOON

Few parents will consider the bassoon. It is a large instrument, not recommended for or chosen by, young children. It is very expensive.

The bassoon is the largest woodwind instrument by far. It is nearly five feet long and every foot costs a lot of money. If a child is really determined to play the bassoon and the money simply is not available to hire or buy one, it is worth "hustling" a little, going from school to school and music centre to music centre to find one available on loan. The favour works in both directions: your child has the instrument without crippling the family budget and the school or music centre fills the bassoonist's chair in the orchestra.

To play any bass instrument requires a good ear, to listen to the higher-register instruments and play harmoniously with them.

Usually adolescent children come to the bassoon as a second instrument after first learning to play a self-contained instrument such as the piano. They feel, or a teacher says, that they now need the experience of playing together with others and are ready to enjoy playing harmony rather than tunes.

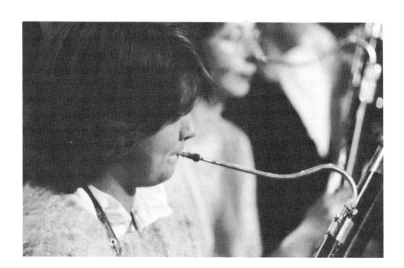

### Physical Suitability

A big and heavy instrument. Although some of the weight is borne by a spike or a sling when playing, few children under thirteen are tall enough, strong enough, have a sufficient finger span and wide enough finger-tips to play it.

The reed is like a very large and thick oboe reed. The player's lips must be folded back to grip it but not as tightly as for the oboe.

Good co-ordination is required as the player can see neither the keys nor his fingers when playing.

### Mental Suitability

No special requirements.

Many slow learners are drawn to the warm sound of this very "human" instrument. The music is comparatively easy to read, but written in bass clef.

### Personality Suitability

"Responsive" or "pleasantly gregarious" are the sort of adjectives that could be used to describe most bassoonists. A quiet sense of humour helps. Indeed, bassoon players tend to be the practical jokers of the orchestra. No good for playing on one's own, the bassoon is essentially an orchestral instrument.

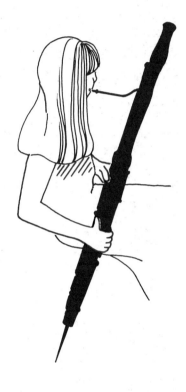

| Suitability Summary | ✓ or ✗ |
| --- | --- |
| Physical | |
| Mental | |
| Personality | |

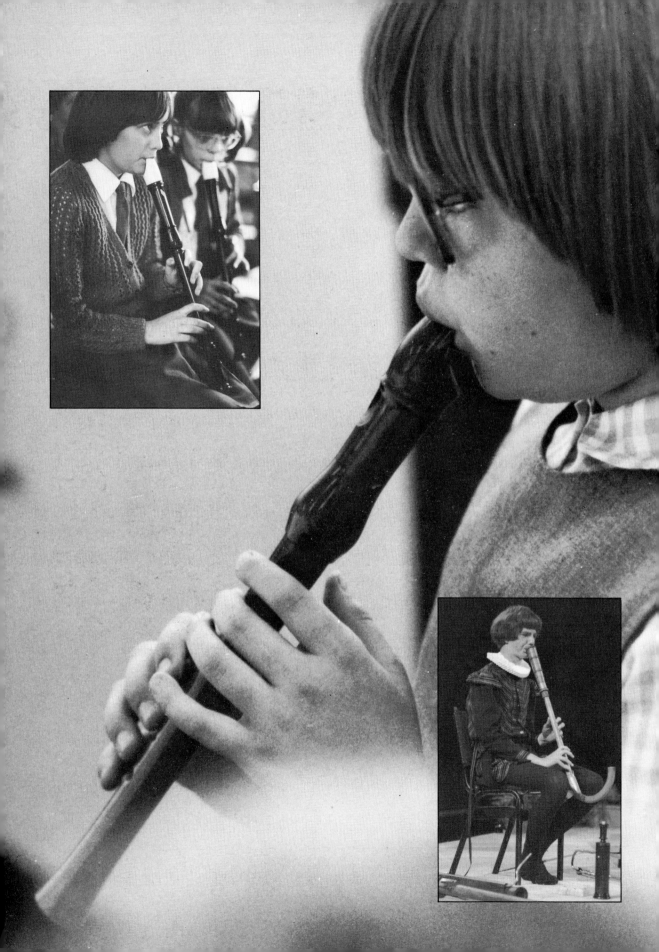

# RECORDER

The recorders are really a whole sub-group of instruments within the Woodwind group. They range from the tiny sopranino, which is very high-sounding, through the descant, treble and tenor recorders to the largest of all: the bass recorder.

Although some schools own the full range, the recorder which is familiar to most children is the descant recorder. It is a simple tube with holes cut in it at precise intervals. Its basic design was evolved tens of thousands of years ago. Primitive people all over the world make and play similar simple instruments. A descant recorder is the cheapest proper instrument you can buy.

The recorder is a real instrument, not a toy. Indeed, advanced recorder technique is extremely difficult. As on all simple instruments—the violin is another example—all the work has to be done by the player, with no valves, keys or other mechanical bits and pieces to make things easier. Unfortunately, there are few music teachers who will give lessons in advanced recorder technique. Most children eventually lose interest in the instrument, if for no other reason, because of the lack of a progressive course of structured lessons.

If few children can learn to play the recorder to advanced levels, almost all children can benefit from the recorder as a preparatory instrument. It is an excellent way to accustom the child to the basic principles of operating an instrument and reading simple notation. Not all children who learn recorder at school get the benefits, however, because the lessons are almost always group lessons, in which a few children learn the instrument—while the others play "follow my leader".

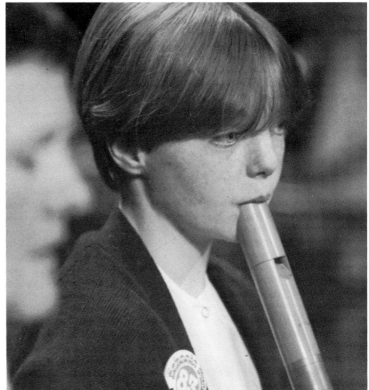

If your child is learning the recorder in group lessons, the recorder can be a very useful indicator for you: as long as the child is happy playing, alone or with friends, the simple repertoire of tunes learnt at school, he or she is not quite ready to start formal lessons on another instrument. The right time to begin proper lessons on a technically more advanced instrument is when the child becomes bored with group lessons, or the technical limitations of the instrument.

## Physical Suitability

Most children find holding the recorder comfortable and pleasurable. A child who does not like putting the recorder in the mouth and keeping it there, or who finds the controlled breathing stressful, cannot enjoy the recorder.

The first fingers used are those of the left hand. The physical co-ordination necessary to play left-hand tunes is within the possibilities of most six-year-olds. The problems arise when, after a few months of learning, it is necessary to co-ordinate individual fingers of both hands, sometimes together and sometimes separately. Many children of eight or nine (and many adults) cannot do this.

Compare the physical difficulty of playing the recorder with both hands and the simplicity of playing a brass instrument with three fingers of one hand only.

Little physical energy is required, or can be released, in playing the recorder. Frail children, including those with respiratory problems, can enjoy the satisfaction of making a musical sound with the minimum of physical exertion. Because it does not release much energy, boys tend to "go off" the recorder earlier than girls.

## Mental Suitability

Most children who are ready to go to school can learn to play simple tunes on the descant recorder, using the left hand only at first.

## Personality Suitability

Children who enjoy singing derive great pleasure from playing the recorder. Boisterous children find the sound of the instrument, and its music, unsatisfying.

Quietly-behaved, gentle children who do well on the descant recorder, move on to the other recorders in junior orchestras, recorder groups and Early Music groups. Here, they can make "real music" in harmonically-structured ensembles.

| Suitability Summary | ✓ or ✗ |
| --- | --- |
| Physical | |
| Mental | |
| Personality | |

59

BRASS

## Thinking about the Brass

You may not have thought about a brass instrument, yet the brass are the instruments of tomorrow for the vast majority of children.

Boys especially are drawn to these shiny powerful instruments, but increasingly girls, too, play the less aggressive, middle-sounding brass.

The advantages of the brass are many:

- any child who can sing or whistle a tune from memory can learn to play a brass instrument;

- beginners' instruments are cheap to buy and are often borrowed free of charge from local bands;

- they are robust and need little looking after apart from cleaning and occasional oiling of the moving parts;

- they last for years and keep their value well for re-sale;

- playing most of these instruments uses only three fingers of the right hand, unlike the piano, or the clarinet, for example, which requires precise co-ordination of all ten digits. Only *very* left-handed children may find this a problem;

- the cost of learning need not be high, for the brass instruments are usually taught in group situations and through bands, rather than by private individual lessons;

- because the whole point of learning a brass instrument is to play it in a band, the instrument automatically gives the child an outgoing, sociable activity—a sort of musical youth club to belong to;

- playing a brass instrument releases a lot of energy otherwise pent up in the telly-addicted child—after a good blow with the rest of the band, you feel good and glowing with health, like after a yoga session or a good game of football;

• there is a brass instrument for every physical build from the small and light cornet to the massive tuba or bass—playing the brass *builds* a healthy body;

• learning the brass can embrace every kind of mentality: quick and brilliant learners have the endless and difficult repertoire of the solo cornet; slow learners, and those who are happy plodding away at the back, are content to play with the other easygoing members of the tuba or bass section;

• thanks to the brass band movement, every kind of music is arranged for brass instruments to play, which means that, whatever kind of music your child prefers, he or she can easily find it arranged for brass—from Early Music through classical and jazz to modern pop and light music.

There are three general disadvantages:

• some children do not like the physical feed-back of vibrating the lips against the mouthpiece and pushing lungfuls of air through the instrument;

• genuinely solitary children cannot take the close physical and emotional relationship in a band (and only the French horn offers satisfaction to the lone learner);

• you must have a local junior band or orchestra or group to play in.

While a parent may think of the brass as one section of a symphony orchestra, modern children are more likely to picture a brass instrument as belonging to a brass or dance band. It is worth distinguishing which brass instruments are played in orchestras and which in brass bands, since you may live in an area which has school orchestras and not bands, or vice versa, and there is no point learning a brass instrument if you cannot get together with others to play it. Some of the brass belong both to orchestra and band, others only in one or the other.

Orchestral brass sections comprise, from small and high-sounding to large and low-sounding: trumpet, French horn, trombone, tuba. In junior orchestras, cornets sometimes play the trumpet part.

A brass band is like a choir. Instead of having voices, it has the smaller, high-sounding instruments to play the tunes, middle-sized and middle-sounding instruments to provide harmony and the large bass instruments for the solid bottom of the sound. From high to low, they are: cornet (which has most of the tunes), tenor horn and baritone, trombone, euphonium, E Flat and B Flat basses.

Also belonging to the brass, but rarely played as first instruments by children, are post horn, coach horn, piccolo trumpet, flugel horn.

The bugle is a marvellous starter instrument for children not quite old enough to begin one of the valved instruments. It is not a progressive instrument because its simple construction restricts it to only five notes, but young children with an urge to play a brass instrument get a lot of fun out of belonging to a marching band for a year or so. This is not a waste of time, for they learn to train both lip and ear, the two essentials for any serious brass instrument—and they have a lot of fun, belonging to their first band.

What a variety to choose from! Most shortlists of children over eight or nine will include one of the brass instruments, unless one of the three disadvantages rules otherwise.

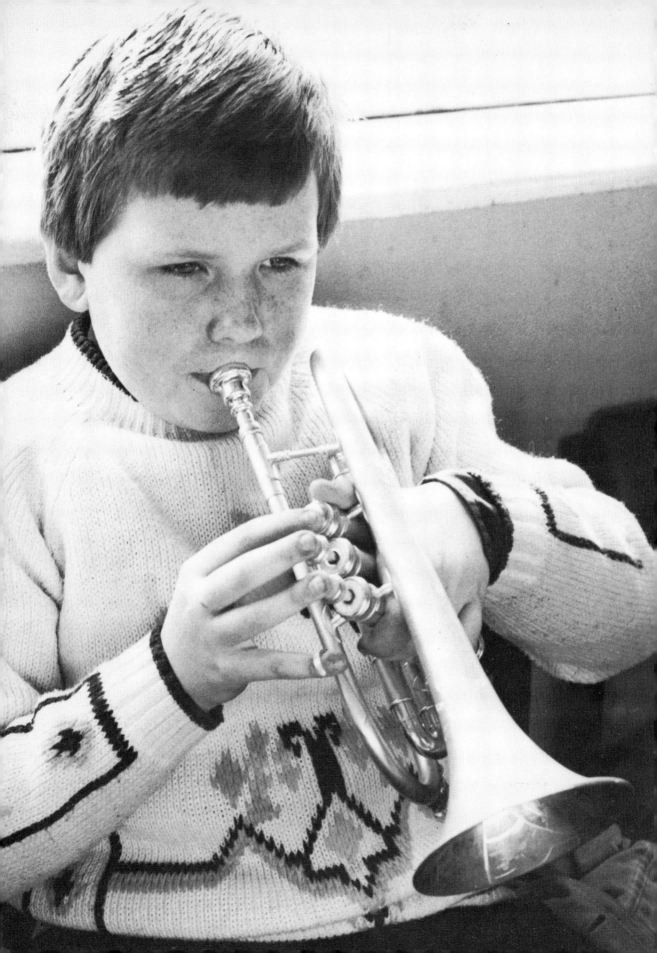

# CORNET

Unless you know about brass bands, you may not even consider the cornet—thinking wrongly that it is just another kind of trumpet.

It is much more than that. The cornet is fun. It is a splendid instrument for children aged eight upwards to learn. It has a pleasing sound, more gentle than the trumpet, is good for playing tunes on and, because it is not physically very hard work to play, is often used as a preparatory instrument for young children who want to learn any of the other brass instruments.

The cornet is more than just a preparatory instrument. It is also the lead instrument of the brass band, as important as the trumpet in a dance band or the first violins in an orchestra.

Brass bands generally are run by energetic, generous people. Players themselves, their main concern is to encourage and help the next generation of players. It is the rule, rather than the exception, that a band will lend an instrument free of charge to a young learner. Most learning is done in rehearsals and band practices rather than in individual lessons. In a junior band, any beginner is welcome to sit in on the third cornet part, playing the one or two notes he or she has mastered and gradually playing more and more as his technique extends. In time, he graduates to the second, and then the solo, cornet sections. The very best players go on to become principal cornets: the stars of the brass band world.

### Physical Suitability

The cornet is light to hold and play. The hands are kept comfortably close to the body. Although looking a little like a short, curly trumpet on the outside, the internal design of the cornet is different, requiring much less "puff".

Asthmatic or bronchial children can benefit greatly from the cornet. Playing it is for them a gentle exercise which builds, rather than strains, the body. Also, they are often very happy to find at last a sociable group activity in which they can take part.

Many a healthy and boisterous seven-year-old may have sufficient energy to blow the cornet, but it is a good idea to wait until the second teeth are firm in the gums before starting to learn properly.

Only three fingers of the right hand are used to operate the valves. Most children find this no problem. Any child who likes the physical feed-back of vibrating the lips and blowing will naturally develop the necessary lip co-ordination. Children who do not like this physical feed-back will never be happy on a brass instrument.

## Mental Suitability

An instrument for both tortoises and hares! The tortoises are happy staying in third and second cornet sections; ambitious hares can race through the stages of technique to the more demanding solo parts.

## Personality Suitability

Most sociable children can enjoy the cornet. The easygoing ones are happy to plod away with the thirds; the aggressive, and dominant or ambitious child (who may later transfer to the trumpet) can find an outlet for his energies in the nervy tension of the solo cornet.

Joining a junior band is an excellent activity for the child who wants to feel independent of the family.

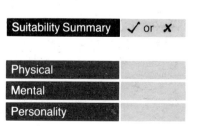

| Suitability Summary | ✓ or ✗ |
| --- | --- |
| Physical | |
| Mental | |
| Personality | |

The trumpet is a powerful, aggressive instrument for out-going, dominant and physically strong children, mainly boys.

Children who want to play a high-sounding brass instrument but who are not dominant or physically strong—or are too young to begin the trumpet—are much better off on the cornet.

All brass instruments are sounded in the same way: the player purses his lips against the mouthpiece and blows a raspberry. This basic sound is then modulated by the size and shape of the instrument—much as the old-fashioned gramophone horn amplified the scratching of the needle on the surface of the record. Distinct notes are produced by tightening and slackening the lips, and by the player depressing one or more valves, or using the slide on the trombone.

The hole in a trumpet mouthpiece is very small, which makes it hard work to force much air through it. At the same time, the instrument is not large and therefore not very efficient at amplifying the sound. To compensate, the player has to strain to force enough air into the instrument. The higher you play, the greater the strain.

Not an instrument for delicate or sensitive children.

It is possible, of course, to play quietly on the trumpet. Indeed, orchestral trumpeters spend most of their time doing so, but that is not the kind of trumpet-playing which attracts many children to the instrument.

Few children will get much satisfaction from learning and playing the trumpet on their own. Trumpeters want to play with, and dominate, others. A junior orchestra gives no outlet for this, so it is important to make sure that the young trumpet-player can find a local junior dance band, show band, big band, or concert band to play in. Remember that the local brass band probably cannot help here (because there are no trumpets in brass bands) although some junior brass bands allow young trumpeters to "sit in" in the cornet sections.

### Physical Suitability

You need energy to play the trumpet—the kind of short-burst energy which makes a football or netball centre-forward. Sheer size is not important. Many children who are a little small for their age feel especially good making a big sound on the trumpet.

The usual age to begin is about ten or eleven. Children starting the trumpet earlier, before teeth and gums are firm, risk deforming their mouths.

### Mental Suitability

You must be alert to play the trumpet: the music has more notes to read and play than the other brass parts. Also, the trumpet is always audible, so any mistakes are obvious to all the other players.

### Personality Suitability

The trumpet is a dominant, or solo, instrument suitable for the *prima donna* temperament. The trumpeter is an independent boy or girl who wants to dominate the sound of the group. He or she has the nerve to play long solos, aiming for success, but also risking failure in front of classmates and friends. This characteristic tends to go with "nervous energy" found in the kind of child who will force him- or herself to go one step further than is safe.

Trumpeters are individualists, who do not belong to the group, but get along well enough with other children—providing they have their full share of the limelight.

| Suitability Summary | ✓ or ✗ |
|---|---|
| Physical | |
| Mental | |
| Personality | |

# TENOR HORN and BARITONE

These instruments, which look like small tubas, are found only in bands. The tenor horn is the smaller, and light to hold and play; the baritone is slightly larger and sounds lower.

These two sections of a band include the highest proportion of girls. You can see from the picture why the boys make jokes about the girls "cuddling their baby tubas".

Learning tenor horn or baritone is a good preparation for the larger and lower brass and the technically more demanding French horn and flugel horn.

### Physical Suitability

These instruments are light and comfortable for boys and girls from nine upwards to hold and play.

These horns demand least energy of all the brass. A little puff into the eggcup-size mouthpiece goes a long way in producing that mellow and gentle sound which is the characteristic of these instruments.

### Mental Suitability

The music is not difficult to read. Other players in the section tend to be helpful, so that even children who are not thought of as bright in school make progress and find they are good at something—and as important as anyone else in the band.

### Personality Suitability

These instruments are very satisfying for gentle children who do not want to dominate or play the tune, but are peaceful, feeling that they belong to a group. They are easygoing, responsive children who like being "in the middle of things"—like the viola-players in the orchestra.

Responsible and never "bossy", they are often asked to become organizers, e.g. the librarian who looks after the band's music, or the Band Secretary who arranges rehearsals, etc.

| Suitability Summary | ✓ or ✗ |
| --- | --- |
| Physical | |
| Mental | |
| Personality | |

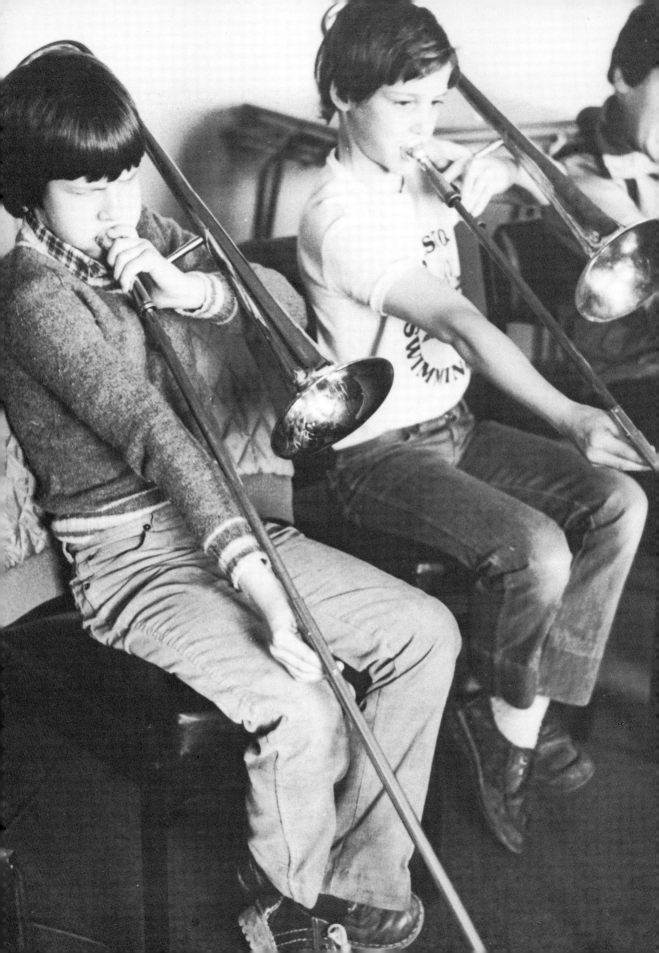

# TROMBONE

The trombone is different from all the other brass. The others are semi-machines and have valves to help find different notes. On the trombone, as on the violin, the player has to form each note, adjusting the position of the slide microscopically to give exactly the "shape" of note he wants. This is very satisfying to an artistic or creative child.

Pushing down the valves of the other brass instruments (their springs push them back up) is a fairly jerky and mechanical exercise, whereas the flowing movements of the trombonist's right arm and wrist are a pleasure for the kind of children who want to move in sympathy with music.

It is a lyrical instrument: children who enjoy singing and the feeling of making music with one's own vocal chords and lungs, yet who like the feed-back of lips vibrating against mouthpiece, will almost always opt for the trombone—as the brass instrument on which you come nearest to singing.

Also, singers have an important advantage. A keen sense of pitch is vital. There are no valves to determine the pitch of the sound mechanically. Therefore, the trombonist must constantly listen to his own sound, control it, monitor the sound of the other players, and adjust his intonation to theirs.

Few parents will be able to assess a child's sense of pitch sufficiently well, but any music teacher can give your child a series of tests, such as the Bentley tests, which tell you whether your child has a sufficiently good ear to play the trombone.

Younger children are naturally attracted to the higher-pitched instruments, which sound roughly in the same register as their own voices. Teenagers, especially tall boys whose voices break early and tall girls who have deeper voices than some of their shorter friends, are similarly attracted by the tenor register of the trombone.

## Physical Suitability

Playing the trombone gives no outlet for the angry energy which makes a trumpeter. The instrument suits physically well-balanced children with the kind of smooth energy which makes good cricketers, ice-skaters or athletes. Although the trombone is very long, it is much lighter to hold and play than you might think.

It is usual to begin learning at about eleven or twelve. Younger children have a problem coping with the right-arm stretches.

The mouthpiece is very much larger than on the cornet or trumpet, requiring more fleshy lips.

This is the only wind instrument (that term embraces both woodwind and brass) which is possible for children with very poor finger control. The fingers do nothing except support the instrument and move the slide in and out.

## Mental Suitability

In a brass band, the trombonist's role is not very demanding. All his music is written in treble clef and he spends his time supplying harmonies to the higher-sounding instruments. In the orchestra, he has to use his brain more, as the parts may be written in any of three clefs (due to the great range of the instrument). However, this is the most versatile of the brass, and the adolescent player who is bored with his orchestral or band role can branch out, according to his musical preferences, into dance bands, big bands, concert bands; he can seek the freedom of improvising in jazz groups or the serious introspection of brass chamber music. Most trombonists are bright and quick-witted and play more than one kind of music with equal pleasure. They are good "all-rounders".

## Personality Suitability

Because each note is "shaped" by the player, this is the brass instrument most fulfilling for artistic children who need to feel they are *making* the sound. Particularly satisfying for the adolescent who wants to express his or her personality playing in jazz bands or other improvising situations.

Most children who succeed on the trombone are quietly sociable, sensitive and artistic.

| Suitability Summary | ✓ or ✗ |
| --- | --- |
| Physical | |
| Mental | |
| Personality | |

77

# EUPHONIUM

The euphonium looks like an overgrown baritone or a stunted tuba. It is more than that, having a soulful quality all of its own. The thought of one of these large instruments being played in a bedroom upstairs while other members of the family have to concentrate on homework or listen to their own music might seem frightening, but the reality is that the sound is quite peaceful and much less disturbing and penetrating than that of the smaller, high-pitched instruments.

The name, euphonium, means sweet-sounding. Today, we expect only high or very loud instruments to play tunes, but in the brass band, the euphonium is the second most important instrument after the cornet. It has its bass, harmonic role but is also in almost every concert a featured solo instrument.

## Physical Suitability

This is an instrument to which children, mostly boys, move on from tenor horn or baritone horn as they grow bigger and can cope with its size and the extra puff needed.

## Mental Suitability

The euphonium suits quietly intelligent children who have a sense of melody and like to feel that they can play tunes on their instrument, yet do not have the aggression necessary for, and are not attracted to, a high instrument.

## Personality Suitability

Responsive children. There is no room in a band for a euphonium player who brashly plays away without listening to the higher instruments.

| Suitability Summary | ✓ or ✗ |
| --- | --- |
| Physical | |
| Mental | |
| Personality | |

"Tuba" is the orchestral name; the same instrument in a brass band is called an E Flat (or B Flat) bass. Whatever it is called, it is big! Yet, it takes less energy to play than the tiny piccolo, or the trumpet. This is because of the way in which brass instruments function: you do not have to fill a brass instrument with air from your lungs each time you play a note, so the sheer size of the tuba places no great demand on the strength of the player; rather the reverse, its size acts as an amplifier, like the old-fashioned gramophone horn.

Where the size is a drawback is in carrying it, transporting it on the bus—and finding a place to keep it in the bedroom.

The single tuba-player in an orchestra can get lonely, but playing E Flat or B Flat bass in a brass band, together with the other basses, is great fun.

**Physical Suitability**
The kind of surplus physical energy that makes a child aggressive is misplaced on these instruments. Many slightly over-weight children who do not have a lot of spare energy are very happy on the tuba.

**Mental Suitability**
You do not need an agile brain. The music is not difficult to read, it is repetitive and you rarely have to play fast. A good sense of rhythm helps a lot and makes playing more pleasurable. The brief solos may not be wildly exciting to listen to, but they are very rewarding to play.

**Personality Suitability**
Responsible, good-natured boys who are happy belonging to a group can be content in band or orchestra playing what seem like endless oompahs to an outsider. It is a bit like being full-back or goalkeeper on the football pitch—a lot of hanging about, but at times you are vital.

| Suitability Summary | ✓ or ✗ |
| --- | --- |
| Physical | |
| Mental | |
| Personality | |

# FRENCH HORN

So far, we have dealt with the brass instruments in order of descending pitch. The French horn is not the lowest-sounding, but has been left until last because it is the most difficult, has little to offer the majority of children and is an exception to most of the generalizations about the brass instruments.

The French horn is not recommended as a first instrument. It is not for fun. It is self-selecting, like the oboe, and appeals to rather similar children.

To produce its distinctive and beautiful sound requires mastery of a technique more difficult than that of any other brass instrument. One position of the player's fingers on the three rotary valves can produce up to twenty notes: only an acute sense of pitch enables the player to conjure the right one out of thin air, by lip control alone.

Almost every child who succeeds on this instrument has previously overcome any problems in reading music through learning the piano or another instrument—or through singing—and desperately wants to play this instrument above all others.

Parental help and encouragement is needed, especially in the early stages. Because the French horn is an orchestral, not a brass band instrument, the child learning has none of that friendly help, encouragement and boosting of morale that comes naturally to other brass learners at their weekly band practice.

French horns are very expensive to buy. Although it is possible to begin with small-group instruction, individual lessons swiftly become necessary for any real progress to be made.

### Physical Suitability

Thin to medium, not generous, lips are called for by the mouthpiece. The small bore through which the air has to be directed produces back-pressure which can cause headaches and dizziness even in quite mature learners. Twelve or thirteen is the conventional starting age.

The French horn is the only brass instrument which develops finger co-ordination for the left hand; the right hand is thrust into the bell to support the weight of the instrument and to help modify the sound.

### Mental Suitability

You can never relax playing the French horn; each note must be *achieved*; there is no letting up.

Any child with a good enough ear and the necessary lip control can succeed. Whether he or she does, depends on willpower and self-discipline as well as intelligence which is needed because the horn is a transposing instrument—indeed, a mental-arithmetic brain helps.

### Personality Suitability

French horn children are not gregarious. Not for them the happy, club-like atmosphere of a brass band. They prefer to relate to small groups and usually have just one or two close friends. The horn-players in an orchestra or concert band make a definite clique and do not mix much even with the other members of the brass section.

Only conscientious, intense children, who have an inner need to work hard and apply themselves over a long period, sustain progress on this instrument. Happier, more easy-going children may—if they have a good ear—begin apparently quite well but give up after reaching the stage of playing a few tunes with the school band, defeated by the difficulties of playing the high and low notes.

The playing position seems to suit, and even comfort, children who feel, rightly or wrongly, that they do not get enough attention at home or school: middle children, for example. With excellent justification, they feel special about playing the horn, for only a very unusual child can.

They may be children who feel that they have under-achieved themselves. They like the noble shape of the French horn, compared with the simple robustness of the other brass instruments. They are naturally possessive of their intricate and expensive instrument and proud to carry it about.

This is probably the only brass instrument which will be practised for endless hours in the privacy of the bedroom. The child who truly wants to be and play alone, is eventually rewarded by an extensive repertoire of music which can be played and practised alone. This is particularly important for a child who for geographical, social or any other reasons cannot go out and play in groups or orchestras.

Children who need the solace of classical music will find a greater potential on this instrument than the other brass.

| Suitability Summary | ✓ or ✗ |
| --- | --- |
| Physical | |
| Mental | |
| Personality | |

STRINGS

## Thinking about the Strings

All the instruments we have looked at so far have one important characteristic in common: the woodwind and brass instruments are for children who have physical energy to use up, by blowing.

Violin, viola and cello are for children with *mental energy* to spare, mental energy which is not absorbed by school, homework, hobbies, etc.

With one exception—the trombone—the "machinery" of woodwind and brass instruments is quite complicated in order to make them easy to play. The construction of the stringed instruments is very simple and they are very difficult to play. Hence the requirement of mental energy.

There never were any easy satisfactions or quick results on the stringed instruments. A couple of generations ago this did not matter, for children were disciplined to work for two or three years at something without expecting any results. Such children could settle down and learn a stringed instrument. Modern children live at a quicker pace and cannot easily defer satisfaction. Most of them *need* the quick results of woodwind and brass.

Unless your child is exceptionally conscientious and patient, it is unlikely that he or she will continue studying a stringed instrument to the point of any real achievement, which takes not months but *several years*.

The child for whom the strings are open to consideration must have spare mental energy, be measurably more musical than most co-evals, have a good sense of pitch, be drawn to classical music, and be very conscientious. For such a child, playing a stringed instrument will become a joy, an enrichment and a source of lifelong spiritual uplift.

# VIOLIN

The violin is a hollow box, made of thin, resonant wood, which amplifies the vibration of one or more of the four tensed strings. The player has to make the string vibrate by scraping sticky horsehair across them.

If that sounds to you like a difficult way of making music, then you are one step along the path to understanding why learning the violin is immensely hard and demands years of dedicated work.

A very good sense of pitch is required. The player makes and shapes each note by "stopping" the strings with the left hand and bowing or plucking with the right. There are no valves, frets, keys or other mechanical devices to help. You need a good ear not only to play the violin, but even to adjust the four strings for each practice session.

Many teachers insist that the parents of young children accompany them to the weekly lessons and take notes in order to supervise the daily practice. This amount of parental involvement, which cannot be skimped, is certainly usual, if not vital for the young learner to succeed.

The violin is the smallest and highest-sounding of the stringed instruments and therefore the one of which the *sound* is most acceptable to young children. It is also the one most commonly available to children as a learning instrument.

Violins are made in three-quarter size, half-size, quarter-size and even one-eighth size, so that there is never a problem in finding an instrument the right size for a child—even from age three upwards. (When buying a small-size violin, you need also a small-size bow to match.)

When assessing the suitability of the violin for your child, it is not important that he or she can hold a small-size fiddle and look comfortable. Rather, think in terms of whether his or her brain is under load from coping with school, or with

new subjects at school. If in doubt, wait, for there is never any reason to hurry a child into learning an instrument.

### Physical Suitability

The instrument suits the light and wiry gymnast or dancer. It is practised standing, which is an exercise in balance for the whole body. It is usually begun by children between the ages of seven and ten on small-size instruments.

The delicate precision required of the player's left hand makes the violin inadvisable for a *heavily* right-handed child. Conversely, most left-handed children can cope with the instrument strung normally.

It is a common misconception among non-players that the violin is supported by the left hand. In fact, the left hand must be free of any weight if it is to do its job of stopping the strings delicately and precisely. The instrument is supported by being gripped between the player's chin and collar-bone. Thus, the vibration of the instrument when being played—which is not discernible to an observer, who only *hears* the acoustically-transmitted sound—passes by bone-conduction

through the child's body directly to the brain. Many children find this vibration unpleasant, even painful. For some children with hearing problems, it can actually be dangerous.

The child who is "right" on the violin is one who finds this bone-conducted vibration positively pleasant and comforting, often a child who for years carried around a favourite toy or a soft blanket as a comforter.

The other form of feed-back from playing the violin is the feeling of "moving with the music" as you play. The child well taught feels the music throughout the whole body. This sensation is particularly satisfying to girls who adore ballet.

## Mental Suitability

Most children who make progress on the violin combine intelligence with sensitivity, a good sense of pitch *and a very high degree of conscientiousness*. Parents may wonder why an obviously bright child who learned quickly to read and write, does well at school and is articulate and socially competent, fails to make progress on the violin and gives up, while apparently less intelligent friends carry on and make progress. The answer is usually that the bright child has found everything too easy and never learned to apply himself. Without conscientious application, sustained progress on the violin is not possible.

## Personality Suitability

Children learning the stringed instruments have no outlet for boisterousness or exuberance. They are quietly behaved children, not solitary but not gregarious either, the sort of children who are quite happy reading in the bedroom or playing with one or two close friends. Even the string-players in an orchestra make only one or two friends; they do not mix with all fifty other members of the strings sections. The great paradox is that they must be able to accept that their principal function as players is to contribute to a corporate sound: the individual string-player is rarely heard alone.

The only child is often drawn to, and does well on, the violin. This is partly because parents spend more time with only children and wish to be involved with their personal development, but also because these children are used to being with, and relating to, adults. Thus they have the ability to form, and benefit from, a close relationship with the teacher, a *sine qua non* of learning the instrument.

| Suitability Summary | ✓ or ✗ |
|---|---|
| Physical | |
| Mental | |
| Personality | |

The viola is a larger version of the violin, similarly strung, but lower, and sounding lower in quality of tone.

If we compare the stringed instruments to a choir, the violins are like the treble voices singing most of the tunes, cellos and double basses are like bass voices providing the solid bottom of the sound and the violas fill the middle.

The viola is rarely the first instrument learnt by a child. Most viola-players have transferred from the violin or another instrument at about twelve or thirteen. Some prefer the lower sound. Others who have progressed reasonably but unexcitingly on the violin opt for the easier music given to the viola (which does not take up so much time to learn, yet still allows them to enjoy playing in the orchestra). Some boys change when their voices break, preferring an instrument whose register is closer to the sound of their adolescent voices.

## Physical Suitability

The viola looks little bigger than a full-size violin, but those few extra inches of length make it *uncomfortable even for many adults* whose left arms are not long enough. The fingers of the left hand have a much wider and more difficult span than on the violin.

## Mental Suitability

Similar to that for the violin, but playing viola parts in the orchestra is less demanding than playing the violin.

## Personality Suitability

Responsive, kindly children who want to contribute to a group endeavour and like classical music, find this instrument and its music very peaceful.

| Suitability Summary | ✓ or ✗ |
|---|---|
| Physical | |
| Mental | |
| Personality | |

# CELLO

Few parents think of the cello as a musical possibility for their children, yet, if there is such a thing as a stringed instrument which is fun for beginners, this is it. Most school orchestras are short of cellists so that any reasonable-standard young player is wanted.

There are three very different reasons for considering the cello.

• At one level, a surprisingly high number of children who have the necessary sense of pitch can become good enough to play the cello to a sufficiently high standard to combine with the higher-pitched strings; the parts are simpler to read, the playing position is easier and the initial sound is not discouraging, as it is on the violin.

• Advanced cello technique required by the concerto soloist or in a string quartet is another matter. It calls for the same degree of applied intelligence and sustained hard work as the violin, and offers similar rewards.

• The third reason is as a "second study". Children already learning the solitary instruments such as piano, organ or guitar often benefit greatly by having to relate to others both socially and musically in orchestras. The cello makes an excellent second instrument in such cases, giving both the feeling of playing a stringed instrument and the experience of orchestral music-making, yet not demanding too much extra practising.

A student cello can be hard to come by, especially in the smaller sizes, and will cost three or four times as much as an equivalent-quality violin. A hard case is a good investment, as cellos are easily damaged.

## Physical Suitability

The playing position is natural and, unlike that for violin or viola, does not have to be learned. The weight of the cello is borne by the spike which rests on the floor. Playing the instrument is pleasantly energetic.

Quarter-, half- and three-quarter-size instruments can be found for children from seven onwards, but despite this the cello is not a satisfactory instrument for children of small or below-average build. The left-hand stretches require large hands. Also the instrument is quite big and heavy to carry about. Few children under thirteen will be able to cope with a full-size cello.

## Mental Suitability

At whatever level the cello is played, it suits a quiet and reflective intelligence.

To progress beyond the level of junior orchestra calls for conscientiousness and sustained hard work—as does the violin. The reward to the child who puts in the necessary years of study is a lifetime of music to play: an inexhaustible repertoire of orchestral, chamber and solo music.

## Personality Suitability

Few young or small children are naturally attracted to a low-sounding instrument like the cello. Children with slightly low-pitched voices, children with larger-than-average chest cavities, children with big hands and long arms—all these find a difficult-to-describe satisfaction when trying the cello. It just "feels right".

Often these children are shy; for them the hidden reward of playing the cello is the quiet and unstressful sociability enjoyed by cellists in group music-making: rarely in the limelight but always respected.

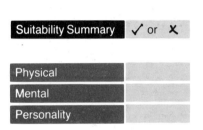

Suitability Summary    ✓ or ✗

Physical
Mental
Personality

# DOUBLE BASS

The double bass is the largest and lowest sounding instrument of the orchestra, providing the rhythmic base of the string sound. Even a small-size double bass is a large instrument, standing higher than the child who plays it.

The instrument has its own attractions for children who have had a basis of learning another instrument, can read bass clef easily and who are *big*.

### Physical Suitability

Sheer physical size which makes an overgrown adolescent feel gawky and embarrassed playing a smaller instrument is a positive "must" for playing the bass. It is important not only to be tall, but also to have large hands with long fingers and a wide finger-span on the left hand. Strength is called for to push that stubby, thick bow across the strings—and to carry the instrument around.

### Mental Suitability

There are no great demands. Written bass music is easy to read and play.

### Personality Suitability

There is no outlet on the bass for a child who wants to dominate, but one who is content to play the simple music well and contribute to the overall balance of the string sections of the orchestra is never short of opportunities to play. Older children with an interest in jazz, or who simply like the idea of playing freely with a few friends, find that plucking the bass in a jazz combo is strangely fulfilling and creatively satisfying, much more so than the casual listener might think.

| Suitability Summary | ✓ or ✗ |
|---|---|
| Physical | |
| Mental | |
| Personality | |

PERCUSSION

## Thinking about the Percussion

The one group of instruments which almost all children have played are those which are hit or shaken: drums, cymbals, triangles, tambourines, wood-blocks—even the baby's rattle.

Most young children enjoy playing with, and on, percussion instruments, as an expression of their innate musicality. During Atarah's Band concerts, hundreds of thousands of children have accepted our invitation to bring along a percussion instrument and join in with the Band. Many adults have been amazed at how seriously and sensitively the children treat their moments of participation in the concert: starting and stopping at the right beat, playing loud and soft as required, playing both simple and complicated rhythms.

School percussion bands can reach high standards and for many children are the high-spot of all their musical experience at school. Playing in these bands is good for a child both musically and socially, yet parents are often baffled as to why there is so little follow-on from the classroom band to a proper course of learning a percussion instrument.

It is precisely because these instruments—or cheap versions of them—are *so familiar* in the primary school, and as toys for little children in the home, that people forget they are real instruments. A proper course of instruction from a qualified percussion teacher can be as rewarding and enriching for the right child as learning the cornet or flute for another kind of child.

There are two kinds of percussion instruments:
*the drums and other un-tuned percussion*
which cannot play tunes but provide rhythm,
and *the tuned percussion* such as
xylophones, chime bars, glockenspiels,
on which tunes can be played.

# DRUMS and other UN-TUNED PERCUSSION

What do you do if your child—at any age from six to sixteen—comes to you and pesters week after week with: "I want to play the drums"? Every group on television, most of the music on radio, whatever he sees and hears, seems to reinforce his interest in the drums and his desire to play them.

In the case of the six-year-old, of course, he *may* just be telling you that he wants to play something. Six-year-olds often pick the drum as their fantasy instrument because it is the easiest one for them to hear: it does not trick their ears by changing pitch like the melodic instruments.

The same child at eight, when he is ready to begin to learn, will have an ear which can identify and appreciate melodic sounds. But the child old enough to begin to learn, and who wants to play the drums, leaves you in no doubt about his suitability. He is probably a hyperactive child—one who is still wide awake at midnight or who rises three hours before the rest of the family.

Any parent with such a child is well-advised to spend time on this section of the book, for taking up percussion seriously has been the salvation of many a hyperactive child.

Learning percussion properly does not mean filling the bedroom with drums large and small and destroying everyone's peace with the thump of bass-drum night and day. A proper course of study begins with just the side drum. A non-drummer rarely understands that a child can happily learn the side-drum for years before needing to go on to other instruments. Indeed, an orchestral percussionist may spend twenty years perfecting his side-drum roll—and still feel that he never played it perfectly!

The side-drum requires regular lessons from a teacher, whether the eventual ambition is to appear on the platform of the Royal Festival Hall in the percussion section of an

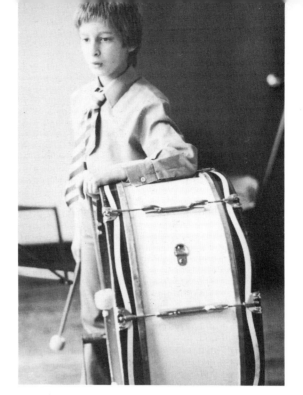

orchestra, or, surrounded by hair, on the scaffolding at a rock festival. Practising between lessons at home can be done with a practice pad over the drum to muffle the sound. Many young drummers are banished to the garage or garden shed, but it doesn't seem to bother them a tenth as much as not being able to practise.

After acquiring a basic technique on the side-drum, the young drummer can move in two directions. If, at thirteen or fourteen, he is beginning to get "into the rock scene", his side-drum technique gives him a head start, for taking up the drumkit.

If he or she is attracted to classical music, or the idea of playing in an orchestra, the young drummer moves on, under the percussion teacher, to learn about the other un-tuned percussion instruments. Each one has its own technique and demands slightly different skills.

In one piece of music the orchestral percussionist may change from playing side-drum to cymbals to wood-block to gong to maracas to bass-drum. What better therapy for the unbearable fidget than to find that his or her natural tendency to drop one thing and immediately pick up another is no longer regarded as a nuisance, but as ideal musical behaviour? (Out of the whole orchestra, only the percussionists stand, move about and constantly change instruments during the music.)

## Physical Suitability

The child who truly wants to play the drums, does more than just talk about it. He drums—with or without music—using his fingers, hands, sticks, knives and forks, on tables, chairs and any surface that comes to hand. He is a real "fidget", who is constantly discharging nervous tension with repetitive small movements.

Drummers are thin, wiry. They often have a huge appetite but never seem to put on weight. They have more stamina than larger, apparently stronger children.

## Mental Suitability

Bright, quick-witted children, who have a natural tendency towards the "butterfly" attitude of starting something and then moving on to the next activity, find a therapy and outlet for their mental energy in percussion. Classroom teachers and parents are often amazed how the child who never settled to anything else can become absorbed in learning percussion technique—practising conscientiously for hours every week over a period of years. What sounds to the untrained ear like two hours of the same beat, is, to a drummer's discriminating ear, a series of subtle variations— what they call, onomatopoeiacally, "paradiddles".

## Personality Suitability

Tense, nervous, often irritable, hyperactive, restless: some of these characteristics are typical of the potential drummer, who is often considerably more independent of the family than other children of the same age.

| Suitability Summary | ✓ or ✗ |
| --- | --- |
| Physical | |
| Mental | |
| Personality | |

# DRUMKIT

Few children younger than thirteen have the extraordinary co-ordination necessary even to begin playing the drumkit. The kit-player may be doing one thing with his right hand, something quite different with his left—and each foot may simultaneously have its own pattern of activity!

The best preparation for a younger child who really wants to learn the kit is to spend a year or two acquiring side-drum technique. He is then far more likely to succeed on the kit than is a child who starts by trying to play simultaneously all the instruments of the kit.

Because many adolescent drummers have prepared themselves badly (if at all) the young drummer who has had lessons on side-drum and percussion technique finds himself welcome not just in rock groups, but also in jazz groups, dance bands, big bands, brass bands—nowadays even occasionally in full youth orchestras when the repertoire includes modern pieces.

A kit-player who can read music and has had basic training can find opportunities to play any kind of music he enjoys.

Suitability Summary   ✓ or ✗

General

# TUNED PERCUSSION and TIMPANI

The tuned percussion include xylophone, chime bars, glockenspiel, also vibraphone and marimba. All these instruments are based on the same logic as the piano keyboard.

Virtually all children who take up these instruments seriously are either pianists who have been learning for several years and are bored or want to be able to join an orchestra or band, *or* are un-tuned percussionists who are required to learn these instruments to play in youth orchestras. Almost never is a serious course of study on these instruments the direct result of playing in junior-school percussion bands. To play tuned percussion properly requires a degree of dexterity and co-ordination extremely rare in children under twelve or thirteen.

The timpani are tuneable drums. Tuning them whilst playing is highly skilled. Drummers with an acute sense of pitch are recommended to transfer to the timps by conductors of school or youth orchestras. These are not first instruments. Virtually no children will succeed on these instruments without prior musical training.

More important than specific physical, mental and personality characteristics are:

- a strong desire to play in band or orchestra;
- a thorough basic training on either piano or un-tuned percussion or any other orchestral instrument;
- above-average dexterity.

| Suitability Summary | ✓ or ✗ |
| --- | --- |

| General | |
| --- | --- |

## Thinking about the Self-Contained Instruments

All the instruments so far considered belong to orchestras or bands, in one or other of the four main suits of instruments: woodwind, brass, strings and percussion. Because they are *designed* for group music-making, few of them offer much to the truly solitary child. Only the flute, violin, French horn and perhaps the cello offer long-term satisfaction to the child who wants to be and play alone.

The jokers in our pack are for solitary children. The piano, guitar and harp are self-contained instruments each of which can play either single notes *or* chords. Thus they can play tunes but they can also provide their own harmonies. (To a limited extent this is also true of the tuned percussion.)

These instruments are difficult. Learning one of them demands far more of a child, mentally, than learning a woodwind or brass instrument but offers in return one distinct reward: from a very early stage, you can play a complete (albeit simple) piece of music, needing no other players for harmony or musical completeness.

The question most often asked by parents is: when is *the right age* to start piano/guitar/harp lessons?

The right age to start is between eight and ten. This is exactly the time when the kind of child suited to the self-contained instruments becomes extremely bored at and by school. Of above-average intelligence, they are among the earliest to be literate and numerate. For them, the first couple of years at school are exciting, but by the third year in primary school they are expected—unless in an exceptional school—to mark time while the less able catch them up.

What happens? These children become bored and lazy. They lose the ability to concentrate and their standards of achievement steadily decline, often to the mystification of teachers and parents alike. The remedy is to give these children something to expand the mentality, the intelligence and the imagination. Learning to play one of the self-contained instruments can do all this.

# PIANO

For many music-lovers a Mozart piano concerto is the epitome of musical beauty. For many young children, the piano itself is a medieval torture-machine. More people have been musically crippled by the piano than by all the other instruments put together.

If that seems a startling statement, ask a few adult friends who had piano lessons (a) how much they enjoyed them, (b) do they still play, (c) did they ever learn to read music fluently, (d) can they still read music . . . and (the crunch question) did it really enrich their lives?

So many people have come to us for counselling about the piano that for many years we were baffled why such a large number of potentially musical, often highly intelligent children and adults had been traumatized to the point of not being able to read a note of music—all by their early experiences on the piano. After analysing hundreds of cases, we found that the majority started lessons between five and seven. This is one of the most stressful periods of a lifetime. The child is busy enough trying to come to terms with school, discipline, other children, having to absorb abstract knowledge, become literate and numerate and so on. The last thing he needs is an additional mental burden during that crucial period.

By far the majority of children put on to the piano at this stressful period build up a mental block about musical notation, about learning an instrument, about their own musical potential. This is a block which can and does last—for most people—for life.

So, what kind of child does succeed on the piano?

## Physical Suitability

Because the piano is a machine which does most of the physical work of producing the sound, it can be played equally well by the frail or the strong. It does not demand physical energy, but rather the reverse: the ability to be comfortable and at ease seated on the piano stool for half an hour or more at a time. Physically energetic children dislike this. Delicate children who are happy to do this, enjoy the power of the sound they can produce on the piano.

Children with less than normal vision—particularly those who wear glasses—find it a considerable strain to read double-clef music (no other commonly learnt instrument has music written in two clefs) and, simultaneously, check visually the changing position of hands and fingers (on no other commonly learnt instrument do the player's hand and finger positions change from the very beginning). The required rapid eye movements and changes of focus demand quite good eyesight. This requirement is rarely borne in mind. Statistically, children with below-average eyesight are less likely to succeed on the piano than those of equal musical potential with good eyesight.

Playing advanced piano music requires precise and complicated co-ordination of all ten digits. However, progress on the instrument is so slow that the pupil develops precise digital control by the time it is required. Children who have learnt the piano for several years make rapid and accurate typists, mechanics, machinists, surgeons. They excel at any activity which requires both hands and several fingers to be used at the same time.

It is sometimes said that a child must be able to span an octave before starting to learn. This is usually an indirect way of saying that the child is too young. In fact, a span of five notes is quite sufficient to start with. Because the piano

is a machine which does the work for you, most children of average physique from five upwards could fulfil the physical requirements sufficiently to begin learning.

## Mental Suitability

The mental requirements are the problem. Few children under the age of eight can satisfy them; few children under the age of eight can appreciate the rewards, either.

A child who is still working hard at reading and/or writing and/or arithmetic, or is experiencing the social pressures of school simply does not have the spare mental energy to come to terms with double-clef notation and all those keys! Such a child only makes apparent progress if "pushed" or helped by a parent at daily practice sessions. Essentially this progress lasts as long as the parent's spare energy. Single children and youngest-in-the family can be taught the piano in this way, because they have a parent who can supply the mental energy which the child lacks.

Reading and playing piano music requires a brain good at mental arithmetic. To such a mentality it is pleasurable to read and decipher two notational codes simultaneously and translate this information into precise finger positions—at the rate of ten to twenty "dots" per second—with different rhythms—with varying pressure—with feet co-ordinated—with intelligence of expression, etc, etc!

To summarize mental suitability for this complicated instrument, the child with a reasonable chance of success on the piano will be:

- at or near the top of the class;
- eight or older, with spare mental energy after all the demands of school have been met;
- good at mental arithmetic;
- naturally conscientious and painstaking;
- possibly beginning to get lazy, waiting for "the others to catch up" at school.

Except for the very, very rare prodigies, progress on the piano is achieved by the steady application of intelligence over a long period.

## Personality Suitability

A quietly intelligent and conscientious child who begins the piano between the ages of eight and ten, is rewarded by a slow but sure series of achievements. Each advance of technique opens new avenues of musical pleasure. At every stage of learning, there is an infinity of music written for the piano—in every possible style from classical to the latest rock.

Gregarious children are miserable on the piano, for it takes many years of study before this instrument can be played with others. Sometimes, however, they transfer to an orchestral or band or group instrument after learning piano for a couple of years. The piano provides an unrivalled basis of musicianship, so these children usually do very well on their second instrument.

The true pianist is a natural loner who likes privacy—perhaps a refuge from the hustle and bustle of older siblings. He or she may be shy, or an exhibitionist, but either way is not the kind to "join in" or want to be part of a group. He or she has an instinctive desire to be self-sufficient.

An only child—or one with very much older brothers and sisters—is used to relating to adults. Such a child is more likely to enjoy and profit from the strong and prolonged teacher/pupil relationship, than a child who is happier with other children and does not relate easily to adults.

Some children are—or feel that they are—"small for their age" get deep satisfaction, and therefore motivation, from the sound they can make on such a powerful instrument. It may be an aspect of this phenomenon that attracts so many young children to the piano, when they are still far too young to begin learning properly.

The piano is too little exploited as a second instrument for older children. Many children begin learning a single-note instrument, but find eventually that the technique is insufficiently demanding or the music unstimulating *for them*. If they are naturally self-contained and have the right mentality, their two or three years' learning on the first instrument enables them to make such good progress on the piano, that, in some cases, they overtake co-evals who began on the piano much earlier. "Late developers" can find this the best route to the piano.

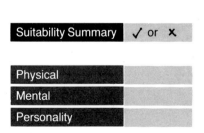

115

# CLASSICAL GUITAR

The classical guitar is an instrument as serious as any in this book. It can be many things to many different children and almost needs a book of its own to explain what it can offer to your child and which kind of children can benefit from it.

There is much to commend it:

● the guitar is a progressive instrument. Its rewards and satisfactions for the right child are equal to those offered by piano or violin. It is as difficult and demanding technically as either of those instruments and therefore pursuing a course of study on the guitar can contribute as much to the child's personal development as learning either of them;

● the guitar has one major advantage for children over piano and violin in that those are the instruments of yesterday, while the guitar is the instrument of tomorrow;

● at any level of learning, there is an endless level of repertoire to play and enjoy;

● it is a quiet instrument delightful to hear coming from the bedroom even on the first fumbling attempts of the youngest beginner—the very first scales sound musical;

● after the initial stages, relatively little parental support is called for, although it is always an excellent idea for parents to listen from time to time to the pieces being worked on, even if the child resists this;

● learning the guitar confers peer-group approval, so important for the child lacking in self-confidence. Few children are ashamed of learning the guitar or give it up because of hostile pressure from school-mates. Boys who live in areas of large cities where they "could not be seen dead'' carrying a violin case find no stigma attached to walking to the weekly lesson carrying a guitar case— thanks to the Beatles and their successors;

• like the piano, it is a self-contained instrument with no need for others to play with and so has a lot to offer the child who through illness, geography or lack of inclination cannot or will not go out and find group music-making opportunities;

• because reading and playing the music is mentally very absorbing but not too demanding physically, the daily practice can be an excellent therapy for asthmatic and other delicate children who need their minds taken off their physical condition;

• an instrument for the beginner is cheap, less than half the cost of an equivalent-quality flute, or a fraction of the cost of a piano;

• unlike the strings or brass, it requires little sense of pitch.

Why then do so many children give up learning the guitar? Anyone reading this book will know that some fail because they are not suited to the instrument, but in the case of the guitar, there is another equally important reason: children and parents alike are hoodwinked by the media into thinking that the guitar is an easy instrument to play and that any happy-go-lucky youth with uncut hair can achieve quick results with no effort.

Nothing could be further from the truth. It takes two or three years of weekly lessons, daily practice and conscientious application to reach the level of playing graded pieces. Luckily many modern children are highly attracted to the guitar and motivated to work much harder at it than they would at any of the orchestral instruments or the piano. However, rarely does a child progress on the guitar without first making a conscious decision to work. The technique of the instrument is difficult, and so also is the music.

## Physical Suitability

Playing the classical guitar (as distinct from folk or electric guitar) uses seven fingers and both thumbs. It develops a quite outstanding degree of digital co-ordination. Children who are good with their fingers—model-builders, girls who like needlework—make a good start.

The player must "stop" up to six strings at a time, using all four fingers of the left hand and simultaneously co-ordinate three fingers and the thumb of the right hand to pluck the correct string or strings with a particular finger or fingers: a degree of physical and mental co-ordination at least as high as that called for when playing the piano with both hands.

Playing the guitar correctly *develops* considerable strength in the fingers, wrists and forearms and for this reason it is often taken up by children who are not robust. The fingers of the left hand must be trained to cope with considerable stretches but the beginner, particularly the younger child starting on a small-size instrument, develops this technique gradually.

To make the playing position as comfortable as possible and avoid bad playing habits which will eventually result in giving up learning, it is important to ensure that children start on a guitar which is not too large. There are three-quarter and half-size guitars to suit children who are physically too small for a full-size instrument.

## Mental Suitability

Whilst young children can be physically comfortable on the small-size guitars, few are mentally ready for the hard work of learning before eight or nine, when the pressure at school is relaxed for a couple of years.

The best progress is made by children who are good at mental arithmetic and good with their hands.

The *genuine* slow-learner (the child who cannot absorb abstract concepts and cannot retain information), or the child whose co-ordination is poor, will not be happy on this instrument. However, sometimes the label "slow learner" is loosely applied to a child who is unhappy in a competitive classroom situation, yet who is naturally methodical and conscientious—in hobbies, for example. Such a child can do far better on the guitar than any school record would suggest. Indeed, many outstanding guitar pupils have poor school reports.

## Personality Suitability

The sound is produced by a repeated plucking motion from the fingers of the right hand. This movement, and the method of holding the guitar close, right in front of the body, seems to be deeply comforting and pleasurable to the acquisitive or possessive child—perhaps a collector, or a hoarder of pocket money.

Chess-players feel good reading and playing guitar music. There is something about the classical guitar and its music (far from the image of flamenco and gypsies etc.) that satisfies the unemotional child, the child who does not want open, or equal-sided relationships. Unlike piano children, who enjoy relating to adults, the guitar-learner is typically self-contained and independent. It is almost a requirement that he should be, because unless a parent or older sibling also plays the guitar, there is no one to whom he can talk about the problems and pleasures of learning and playing this instrument. The weekly visit to the guitar teacher is just about the only time in the week when the child can "open up".

The child who succeeds on the guitar enjoys being alone, wants to be independent and will work hard and determinedly to achieve independence. There are few opportunities for group music-making on the guitar.

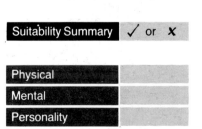

| Suitability Summary | ✓ or ✗ |
| --- | --- |
| Physical | |
| Mental | |
| Personality | |

If many parents overlook the guitar, few indeed will ever think of the harp. How many modern homes even have space for an instrument five feet high and four feet wide? How many children want to pluck 46 strings using two thumbs and eight fingers and operate seven pedals using both feet? As if that's not enough, the 46 strings all have to be tuned—by the player!

Well, some children hear a harp or see it on television perhaps for the first time and just *know* this heavenly instrument is for them.

No child is ever in two minds about learning the harp. It is not a candidate for many shortlists. The would-be harp player will tell Mum and Dad again and again and again that this is the one instrument which he or she wants to play. What do you do about it? You cannot just walk into the local music shop and buy one. Even when you have found a harp, it will have a price ticket to make you gasp: several hundred pounds for an old one which needs attention and several thousand for a good new one.

What do you do if it is going to be two or three years before your child can have one? The best preparation meanwhile is to learn the piano. While not physically satisfying, this familiarizes the child with treble and bass clef notation, as read by a harpist.

Most harp children begin—especially in Wales—on the smaller, cheaper and easier-to-play Celtic harp which has only 29 strings, is easily portable and has no pedals to bother a beginner. Only very self-contained shy children, mainly girls, will want to spend many hours a week practising either Celtic or orchestral harp. No parent can help much except by providing occasional transport (for lessons, you use the teacher's harp or, in Wales, the school instrument). An orchestral harp takes two adults to manoeuvre into one of the larger estate cars.

What are the rewards? Solo harp music is transcendently beautiful to play and listen to; the harp is a wonderful instrument to accompany the human voice—either the player's or a friend's; and, if you have transport, any youth orchestra for older children will welcome a harpist.

It is difficult to find anyone to give advice about the harp, for few schoolteachers, Music Advisers or even professional musicians know anything about it, so, if your child passionately wants to play it, write to your nearest professional orchestra and ask the harpist to give you and your child some advice before or after a rehearsal. Do not expect written advice. You will have to be prepared to travel and be there when it suits the harpist's busy schedule, but it is the only way. Harpists are fanatical about their instrument as well as being extremely helpful people. Few of them will turn down a polite and reasonable request for help—after all, they know the problems you have.

| Suitability Summary | ✓ or ✗ |
|---|---|

| General | |

SELF-TAUGHT INSTRUMENTS

**Thinking about the Self-Taught Instruments**

All the instruments so far examined have one thing in common: they are learnt formally. Children study them by following a progressive course of structured lessons under the tuition of trained teachers, with progress measured by regular examinations. The child knows how well he or she is doing. A succession of achievements in graded exams builds the child's confidence. The child is able to understand the relationship between work and results, which leads to an early development of self-discipline. Learning an instrument in this way contributes much to the child's developing character.

There are no such advantages for children on the self-taught instruments. They are learnt informally: by ear, by trial and error, by painstakingly copying the sounds heard on cassettes and records. It is rarely possible to find lessons. When tuition is available, it is usually given by an older amateur player, not a trained teacher, who may—or may not—have evolved his own pattern of learning the instrument. Most players cannot read music.

Whilst few children can succeed in learning an instrument in this manner, many adolescents need to be free from adult teachers. They want to achieve something by their own efforts and with some help from friends. They want informality and independence and are prepared to devote great energy to what is, comparatively, a far more difficult way of learning an instrument.

# ELECTRIC GUITAR

All electric instruments—guitar, bass and keyboards—are designed to make a lot of noise. They can be played quietly, but what sounds quiet to the player can be intolerably loud to the other occupants of the house. Most of the music they play—and this is the reason why adolescents want them—is as aggressive and masculine as a motorbike. The problem even for the young player who has promised to practise quietly is similar to that of the motor-cyclist who has undertaken not to exceed 15 m.p.h.—it is too unsatisfying.

This instrument is not hollow like the classical guitar. It is solid and heavy to hold and play. The weight burden and the stretches required of the left hand make it uncomfortable for most children until about thirteen, although younger children *determined* to play it will put up with a great deal of discomfort, such is the appeal of these instruments. The fingertips of the left hand can become very sore from pressing against the steel strings.

Junk shops are full of guitars abandoned by once-hopeful children who were too young to start or who thought it was all going to be so easy. The player must practise for many hours a week to acquire the co-ordination of right and left hands. The music is rarely written and proper teaching is almost impossible to find. Teaching yourself to play even a few chords by ear is hard.

The musical miracle of these instruments is not that so many give up, but rather that so many persevere on their own to the stage where they can begin playing with friends. It is a pity that the school system has little interest in, or way of recognizing, this hard work, and does little to help.

That all sounds so negative, but before you heave a sigh of relief that all your worst fears and prejudices have been confirmed, let us ponder what good these instruments do, what they have to offer your child in terms of personal

development. Surprisingly, quite a lot.

Most adolescent boys need to get away from parents, teachers, siblings and even girls of their own age. They need a valid reason to get together with other young males in self-organized groups doing something masculine. Playing an electric instrument or the drumkit in a group does all this *and* it confers status in the eyes of school-mates. If you and the family can somehow cope with the noise problem, this hobby can make a teenage son *easier* to live with, giving him always "something to do", the physical pleasure of playing a powerful instrument, a development of nervous and muscular co-ordination, the satisfaction of making musical progress, a sense of achievement which builds identity, an ever-present relief from the tensions of adolescence and a wonderful way of making new friendships.

If a child younger than eleven or twelve insists that he wants to play the electric guitar, what does a parent do?

Well, it must be borne in mind that these instruments contain live mains voltage, which can kill. The player inevitably takes guitar and amp to pieces, changes parts, cures problems. This is obviously dangerous if the child is too young to understand electricity. Also, the instrument and its necessary amplifier cost more than many parents are prepared to spend on them.

We suggest in these circumstances that the child be encouraged to start saving pocket-money towards the cost of instrument and amplifier, whilst, at the same time, beginning lessons on either a single-note instrument or the classical guitar—as a preparation for the electric guitar.

| Suitability Summary | ✓ or ✗ |
| --- | --- |
| General | |

128

# BASS GUITAR

Every teenage rock-group needs a good bass-player. Many school bands, brass bands, big bands and dance bands use a bass guitar instead of the old-fashioned (and often inaudible) double bass. Any teenager who has learnt to read bass clef on piano, cello, double bass or bassoon can pick up a bass guitar and within a couple of weeks be launched on an exciting new hobby. The electric guitar requires chordal technique; the bass plays only one note at a time. What music exists is easy to read and play.

Like all the other bass instruments, the bass guitar is frustrating for the aggressive extrovert. For a tall, responsive adolescent who does not want to hog the limelight yet wishes to have a ready passport to rock group or band, it is a wonderful Christmas or birthday present.

| Suitability Summary | ✓ or ✗ |
| --- | --- |
| General | |

# ELECTRIC KEYBOARDS/ORGANS

Many an adolescent who has been progressing satisfactorily on the piano for several years suddenly loses interest overnight.

The negative parental reaction is to insist that lessons be attended and practice done, because all that childhood effort "cannot be thrown away". A more positive reaction is to think of investing in an electric keyboard, which can give the young player the kinds of freedom so important to a teenager—to improvise, harmonise with one's own voice, play with friends in informal groups—and use what has been learnt on the piano as a social attribute during the difficult years of adolescence.

There is a wide range of these instruments which can be played and enjoyed by the child who has persevered to Grade Five or Six on piano. Manufacturers' publicity that suggests the instruments are suitable for children without prior knowledge of keyboard technique, or at least the ability to read music, should be treated with proper parental suspicion.

Suitability Summary    ✓ or ✗

General

# FOLK GUITAR

Some teenagers are naturally quiet individuals. Not for them the aggressive atmosphere of a rock group, nor the unavoidable sociability of a folk club. Yet, between fifteen and twenty, they begin to feel that they have missed out on music by not having proper lessons on an instrument during childhood, or by having given them up.

The folk guitar, played solo or accompanying their own or a friend's voice, can be the answer. This is a light, hollow-bodied acoustic instrument. It looks like a large classical guitar, but the strings are made of steel, to give a louder, harsher sound.

It takes a reasonably good ear to progress beyond the level of a few basic chords and a good musical instinct to improvise harmonic accompaniments—about the same as shown by Grandad when he used to bang out "songs from the shows" on the drawing-room piano. The capo is a device clamped on to the strings to make playing easier. Lessons are rarely obtainable, but, because the instrument is widely self-taught by people of all ages, there are many excellent tutor-books on the market.

Some junior schools offer folk guitar group lessons, in which the children learn a few basic chords and to pick out a small repertoire of tunes. This is nothing like studying classical guitar technique. However, a child who enjoys these group lessons, who wants to learn the guitar properly and who satisfies the three-way suitability criteria, has a good motivation to begin learning classical guitar.

Suitability Summary ✓ or ✗

General

131

Some adolescents continue to enjoy and need the company of adults and younger siblings. For them, the exclusively youth-orientated rock group is not so attractive.

The easy-going informality of folk music may be what they seek. Members of local folk clubs are pleasant and friendly people. The players and singers, who are mainly non- or semi-professional, are helpful. There are opportunities to hear a surprising range of instruments playing a wide range of music—and talk to the players, who may help to find instruments and be prepared to give advice.

The instruments include folk fiddle, acoustic and electric guitars, string and electric bass, dulcimers, lutes, drums, tambourines, recorders, Celtic harps, accordions (both piano and button), whistles, flutes and many traditional instruments such as the bagpipes.

To learn an instrument by ear takes a lot of patience and application, but it can be done by a well-motivated adolescent. Those who learned another instrument for a couple of years in childhood can do well. Within months, they can be performing their first "numbers" to as nice and appreciative an audience as can be found anywhere.

Easy-going, sociable youngsters are always welcome at folk clubs.

Ethnic music is different. This category includes Irish bands, steel bands, Asian dance groups, marching bands. The clubs usually specialize in one kind of music, which is secondary to the main purpose of bringing together and keeping together people from a common cultural background.

Suitability Summary    ✓ or ✗

General

Because so few children hear or see fretted instruments being played, they do not commonly figure on lists of "Instruments I Should Like To Play". (Frets are the thin bars fixed across the neck of guitars, banjoes, mandolins and other plucked and strummed instruments.)

This group of instruments includes:

- banjoes, ukeleles;
- mandolins, lutes;
- various regional and national plucked and strummed instruments; for instance, the balalaika.

These instruments had a great vogue of popularity before skiffle and electric instruments ousted them from fashion. Now, the Federation of Fretted Instrumentalists is working hard to bring them to a wider public.

Yet, some children hear these instruments for the first time and are instantly attracted by the sound. They "just know" that the mandolin, or the . . . is the instrument they have been looking for. Mostly, the fretted instruments appeal to older children who like the "atmosphere" of a banjo band, a ukelele orchestra or a lute group, without quite knowing why.

What kind of children are they?

They are generally quiet in behaviour and voice. Introspective but not withdrawn. Intelligent, but not sharp or bright. "Good with their fingers". Patient and conscientious. Subject to enthusiasms, sometimes collectors.

These instruments are satisfying to practise and play at home, because both melodies and chords can be played on them. They are not noisy, which can be a great advantage in thin-walled modern accommodation. Played in groups, they have the quiet intensity of a chamber orchestra.

Because most of the music is specially arranged for the ensemble, the repertoire is as wide as the players want it to be. The clubs and bands are organized by devoted amateurs. Help in finding instruments, guidance and some kind of lessons can usually be obtained through the club or band.

Except for the largest, bass, instruments, all the fretted instruments are comfortable to hold and play.

A few solitary adolescents take up mandolin or lute as a solo instrument, learning to play by ear only. To play in any kind of group, however, necessitates learning to read music. As in the brass band, this does not seem to be a problem for the well-motivated. They "pick it up as they go along".

Suitability Summary ✓ or ✗

General

# PART 3: FINALIZING THE CHOICE

Your child's Short List is now made up of the small number of instruments which have no cross on their Suitability Summary. One of them is the Right Instrument. So close, and yet so far? Not at all—getting rid of the others until only the Right One is left, is the easiest stage of the whole process. In fact, your child does most of the work, as you will see.

The majority of children's Short Lists have only two or three instruments. Reducing them to the Right Instrument is done with the child. However, it is possible that you have five, or more, instruments which have no crosses against them. If so, you have an intermediate stage to carry out, *before involving the child.*

**Reducing the Short List—without the Child**

Eliminate the marginal instruments in the following order:

1. The instruments which sound least like your child's voice. (This may seem a strange idea when you first read the words, but it makes sense. Children are naturally and instinctively attracted to those instruments which sound approximately in the same register as their own voices. This explains why so many children are drawn to the treble instruments such as flute, recorder, clarinet, cornet, violin. Many young children find it hard to hear bass, or low-sounding instruments and no child can be highly motivated to learn an instrument which is hard for the player to hear.)

2. Instruments which would be too expensive to buy or hire. (Bassoon or harp, for example, are outside most family budgets.)

3. Instruments too large to have in the home, or to transport. (Piano, tuba, double bass, harp may simply be too cumbersome for many modern houses and flats.)

4. Instruments (other than self-taught) for which there are no lessons available locally. (Your music shop or public library can give you information.)

*Tick only those instruments which have no crosses
on their Suitability Summary.*

**Woodwind:**

- Flute
- Clarinet
- Saxophone
- Oboe
- Bassoon
- Recorder

**Brass:**

- Cornet
- Trumpet
- Tenor Horn/Baritone
- Trombone
- Euphonium
- Tuba/E Flat/B Flat Bass
- French Horn

**Strings:**

- Violin
- Viola
- Cello
- Double Bass

**Percussion:**

- Drums/Un-Tuned Percussion
- Drumkit
- Tuned Percussion/Timpani

**Self-Contained Instruments:**

- Piano
- Classical Guitar
- Harp

**Self-Taught Instruments:**

- Electric Guitar
- Bass Guitar
- Electric Keyboards/Organs
- Ethnic/Folk Instruments
- Folk Guitar
- Fretted Instruments

By the time you have eliminated these four categories of marginal instruments, the Short List should be manageable. The next stage is done by you and the child together.

### Reducing the Short List—with the Child

You and the child go to the largest, or the most friendly, music shop in the area and try all the instruments on the Short List. It's as simple as that.

The staff will help, by showing your child how to assemble the instruments properly, how to hold them and how to produce a note. If the child is shy, they can usually find a private cubicle or studio at the back of the shop where he or she can try the instruments without embarrassment or distraction.

The child will tell you which one feels nice and which does not; which is too heavy or too large to hold, or demands too much energy to play; which "makes a nice sound"—in short, which is the Right One.

The parent's only problem is that, having done so much hard work to get to this stage, it is tempting to interfere when the child is trying the instruments. Be content with a background role. You are there just to deal with the assistants in the shop. Your child is in charge of the selection itself.

At our Music Centre, we frequently had a hundred or more children trying their Short List instruments on a single day. Almost all of them just knew that they did or did not like the violin/cornet/flute by the simple expedient of holding it (under guidance) and producing a few notes on it.

Some children may be luke-warm about one or two instruments, but all children can quickly say which instruments they either like or do not like—provided the parent does not make suggestions. It can be difficult to avoid "loaded" questions like: "That's a lovely violin. Did you like it?" To this sort of question, most children try to give the answer they think the parent wants.

Buying a musical instrument is—at any age—a very personal matter. Let the child take as much time as he or she wishes. Don't restrict the try-outs to one go on each instrument. Your child—as the potential owner of a real musical instrument—deserves V.I.P. treatment in any music shop. You will find that the staff understand the problems. They would far rather sell you the Right Instrument after three or four visits, than a wrong one on the first day you go into the shop.

A musical instrument is not just another toy. The Right Instrument may be the most important possession you ever buy for your child.

Ahead of you both lie many magic moments: the first experimental notes, the first recognisable tune, "real" music, examination successes, Festivals, public performances, joining an orchestra or band. Who knows where this could lead? A life-time of music-making is made possible by the time and thought which you devote to choosing the Right Instrument for Your Child.

# Appendix

## Buying or borrowing an instrument

Professional musicians spend hundreds, even thousands, of pounds on their instruments, but the 'student' instruments on which children begin to learn cost far less. They are priced by the manufacturers to be within range of the average family budget. While there is little chance of getting a bargain on a particular model by shopping around, it is worthwhile to visit several music shops, since they do not all have the same range of instruments on offer.

Because the international musical instrument market is very competitive, prices are a guide to quality. In general, the more you pay, the better the instrument. The very cheapest instruments may have defects which will handicap the learner, or at least cause dissapointment. If subsequently, you wish to sell the instrument, or to trade it in for a better one, the additional investment to buy a better instrument in the first place, will more than be justified. Unlike toys or domestic applicances, proper musical instruments hold their value well, the better ones even appreciating as time goes by. Electric instruments, on the other hand, lose value overnight—like a new car. When buying outright, it is quite usual to ask for, and be given, one week's approval, in order to have the instrument vetted by the teacher.

Many parents prefer not to buy outright. Any reputable music shop will offer two other possibilities. Hire purchase is as normal for instruments as for refrigerators and television sets. Peculiar to music is the hire-and-buy system, whereby you hire the instrument from the shop for three or six months and the hire fee is deducted from the purchase price if you eventually decide to buy. The advantages are obvious. Of the three ways to obtain a new instrument, this is the one we recommend.

Most music shops also have a selection of used instruments. The prices may not be lower than for new models, but you should get better value for money—in other words, a better quality instrument—when buying a guaranteed second-hand instrument from an established music shop.

Buying privately is a more risky business. Most local papers carry advertisements for private sale of used instruments and local junk shops often have musical instruments displayed in the window. If you do find what seems to be a bargain in either of these ways, it is worth paying a small fee to your local music shop, or a teacher or musician, to examine the instrument before purchase is completed. Many defects are not obvious to the layman, nor even to players of other instruments, yet can be a crippling disadvantage to the child beginner.

It is in some areas possible to borrow an instrument long-term through the school system. This can be a good idea, in order to get started before funds are available for purchase. However, such loaned instruments have often been damaged or neglected by a previous borrower. They should always be thoroughly overhauled by a trained repairer before the child begins to learn.

Lastly, brass bands normally lend instruments long-term to any child who joins the junior section.


## Finding a teacher

Depending where you live, it can be easy or difficult to find a teacher for a particular instrument. Teachers of the 'traditional' instruments like piano and violin are more widely available than their colleagues who specialise in giving, say, french horn or saxophone tuition. Most music teachers belong to one of two organisations:

The Incorporated Society of Musicians, at 10, Stratford Place, London W1

The Music Teachers' Association, at 106, Gloucester Place, London W1

Your local Public Library should have a list of music teachers in the area. Yellow pages list both music schools and individual teachers. Local music shops usually keep a list of teachers and, in many cases, have studios on the premises where lessons are given.

Some Area Educational Authorities offer group instrumental lessons. Enquire at the child's school or to the office of the Music Adviser. Normally, these lessons are restricted to those instruments for which teachers happen to be available within the system.

If your child's Right Instrument is one for which there is not a great demand locally for tuition, it is unlikely there will be a full-time teacher. Partly for this reason, most professional musicians also teach. The national office of the Musicians' Union at 60/62, Clapham Road, London SW9, will give the address of the area office, from which you can obtain a list of members who play the instrument in question. The added glamour of learning from a player can be a source of motivation for the child.

Similarly, any mature music student should be equipped to teach children. It is quite normal to contact a Music College, University or Polytechnic Music Department and ask for the names of students who teach.

Good luck!